Caledonia

by

Alistair Beaton

Lyrics by Alistair Beaton

(some based on ballads of the time)

T0258368

B L O O M S B U R Y

LONDON · NEW DELHI · NEW YORK · SYDNEY

Bloomsbury Methuen Drama
An imprint of Bloomsbury Publishing Plc

50 Bedford Square   1385 Broadway
London   New York
WC1B 3DP   NY 10018
UK   USA

www.bloomsbury.com

Bloomsbury is a registered trade mark of Bloomsbury Publishing Plc

First published 2010

© Alistair Beaton 2010

Alistair Beaton has asserted his right under the Copyright, Designs and Patents Act, 1988, to be identified as author of this work.

All rights reserved. No part of this publication may be reproduced or transmitted in any form or by any means, electronic or mechanical, including photocopying, recording, or any information storage or retrieval system, without prior permission in writing from the publishers.

No responsibility for loss caused to any individual or organization acting on or refraining from action as a result of the material in this publication can be accepted by Bloomsbury or the author.

All rights whatsoever in this play are strictly reserved and application for performance etc. should be made before rehearsals by professionals and by amateurs to Alan Brodie Representation Limited, Paddock Suite, The Courtyard, 55 Charterhouse St, London EC1M 6HA. No performance may be given unless a licence has been obtained.

No rights in incidental music or songs contained in the work are hereby granted and performance rights for any performance/presentation whatsoever must be obtained from the respective copyright owners.

Visit www.bloomsbury.com to find out more about our authors and their books You will find extracts, author interviews, author events and you can sign up for newsletters to be the first to hear about our latest releases and special offers.

British Library Cataloguing-in-Publication Data
A catalogue record for this book is available from the British Library.

ISBN: PB: 978-1-4081-3627-0
       EPDF: 978-1-4081-3629-4
       EPUB: 978-1-4081-3628-7

Library of Congress Cataloging-in-Publication Data
A catalog record for this book is available from the Library of Congress.

Caledonia was first performed at the King's Theatre, Edinburgh, on 21 August 2010, in a co-production between the National Theatre of Scotland and the Edinburgh International Festival. The cast, in alphabetical order, was as follows:

Reverend Francis Borland	Paul Blair
Robert Blackwood	Tam Dean Burn
King William of Orange	Cliff Burnett
Joost	David Carlyle
James Balfour	Alan Francis
Mrs Paterson	Frances Grey
William Paterson	Paul Higgins
John Erskine	Neil McKinven
Ensemble	Robert Melling
Roderick Mackenzie	Matthew Pidgeon
Ensemble	Morna Young

Nameless of the Earth, MPs, Merchants, Subscribers, Clerks, Councillors, Sailors, Colonists, Servants and all other parts played by the Company.

Writer   Alistair Beaton
Director   Anthony Neilson
Designer   Peter McKintosh
Composer/Musical Supervisor   Paddy Cunneen
Musical Director   Robert Melling
Lighting Designer   Chahine Yavroyan
Sound Designer   Nick Sagar
Movement Director/Assistant Director   Anna Morrissey
Casting Director   Anne Henderson

About the National Theatre of Scotland

Scottish theatre has always been for the people, led by great performances, great stories and great writers. As Scotland's national theatre, we exist to work collaboratively with the best companies and individuals to produce and tour world class theatre.

Our ambitions are simple: to create work that excites, entertains and challenges audiences at home and beyond and which makes Scotland proud. We're a theatre company with an adventurous streak and at our heart is a strong desire not to do things conventionally.

Everything we aspire to challenges the notion of what theatre can achieve. With no building of our own we're free to make theatre wherever we can connect with an audience.

For the latest information on all our activity visit our online home at www.nationaltheatrescotland.com

National Theatre of Scotland
Civic House,
26 Civic Street,
Glasgow G4 9RH
T: +44 (0) 141 221 0970
F: +44 (0) 141 331 0589
E: info@nationaltheatrescotland.com

The National Theatre of Scotland wishes to thank the following individuals and organisations for their support.

Crerar Hotels
Inchyre Trust
JarHair
Leeds Building Society
Merchants House of Glasgow
Mr Boyd Tunnock
Mrs Katharine Liston
Mr Martin Segal
Miss E.C. Hendry's Charitable Trust
Nancie Massey Charitable Trust
Tayfield Foundation
The Alma and Leslie Wolfson Charitable Trust
The Binks Trust
The Craignish Trust
The Endrick Trust
The Hugh Fraser Foundation
The Pleasance Trust
The RJ Larg Family Trust
The Roger & Sarah Bancroft Clark Charitable Trust
The RS Macdonald Charitable Trust
The Robertson Trust
The Russell Trust
Two Fat Ladies Restaurants
Schuh
ScottishPower
Talteg Limited
Tayfield Foundation
Union Advertising Agency

The Scottish Government

The National Theatre of Scotland is core funded by the Scottish Government. The National Theatre of Scotland is a registered Scottish charity SCO33377.

Preface

Caledonia is a story of greed, folly and mass delusion. In that respect it is a very modern tale. But it is also a darkly tragic and fitfully heroic tale of its time.

In the 1690s, Scotland – still an independent nation despite a shared crown with England – decided it wanted to be a colonial power. That great Scottish visionary, charmer and financier William Paterson was the moving spirit behind the decision to set up a colony on the isthmus of Panama. He dreamed that Scotland would thereby control the trade between East and West and virtually overnight be transformed from a small, poor nation into one of the world's major economic powers. There was every reason to believe him; this was, after all, the man who just a few years earlier had founded the Bank of England. The atmosphere was also propitious: the growing popularity of that recent invention the joint stock company persuaded people that there were new and virtually risk-free ways of making vast amounts of money.

Paterson's plan for a Scottish colony was greeted with nationwide enthusiasm. Subscription books were opened in Edinburgh and Glasgow and within weeks the Scottish people had invested a vast proportion of their wealth.

The vision may have been soaring, but the execution was prosaically bad. Virtually every danger had been underestimated. Perhaps two thousand settlers died from disease, hunger and skirmishes with Spanish troops. Nor had Paterson reckoned with the implacable opposition of King William and the English Parliament. Despite sending two mighty fleets, Scotland was soon forced to abandon the colony, which in a moment of grandeur and hope, had been named Caledonia.

The catastrophe left Scotland fatally weakened and led a few years later to the end of Scotland as an independent nation.

Following the Treaty of Union with England in 1707, cartloads of money were sent up to Scotland to pay off the shareholders of the Company that had been responsible for the disaster.

Every history play has to strike a balance between historical truth and dramatic truth. To make the subject work as a play I had to simplify some incidents, change the order of some events, and create a mixture of invented and historically real characters. What is astonishing though, is how many of the details of the story strike a chord with today's world of finance without my having to alter a word. This echo of today extends even to Paterson's use of lavish hospitality to win over the Great and the Good.

That is why *Caledonia* is a Scottish story, an international story, an ancient story, and a modern story.

Alistair Beaton
July 2010

Caledonia

Principal Characters

William Paterson
Roderick Mackenzie
James Balfour
Robert Blackwood
John Erskine
Mrs Paterson
Reverend Francis Borland
Robert Pennicuik

A chorus of the Nameless of the Earth

Other Characters

Innkeeper
Members of the Parliament of Scotland
First Serving Maid
Second Serving Maid
Serving Boy
The Marquis of Tweedale
Sergeant-at-Arms
King William of Orange
Joost
Town Crier
Flunkey
Foreign merchants
Servant to William Paterson
Various servants
Directors of the Company of Scotland
Lionel Wafer
Clerks
Subscribers
Drunks
Councillors of the Colony
James Smyth, merchant
Servant to James Smyth
Poor girl

Sailors
Lookout
Colonists
Captain Aguillon
Gravediggers
Ship's boy
Servant to Balfour and Blackwood
Banker

Act One

Scene One – The Ship Tavern, Edinburgh, the late seventeenth century

Curtain up or lights up on **Paterson**, *dictating to an* **Innkeeper**, *who proceeds to follow him obsequiously round the room, writing everything down.* **Paterson** *is thinking up his order as he goes. To one side of the stage stands* **Mackenzie**, *a leather-bound ledger under his arm. Hanging from the set (which should be constructed to permit climbing) downstage left and downstage right are the miserably attired* **Nameless of the Earth**. *They silently observe the action. For the other characters on stage, the* **Nameless** *do not exist.*

Paterson I want it to be just right, do you understand? Everything . . . just right.

Innkeeper Of course, Mr Paterson. I have reserved the private dining room on the first floor.

Paterson Very good.

Innkeeper And as to the menu, we can offer –

Paterson Yes, yes, thank you. We will have . . . um . . . five pound of herring.

Innkeeper Very good, Mr Paterson. Five pound . . . of . . . herring.

Paterson Three lobsters. No, better make that four. Four lobsters.

Innkeeper Four lobsters.

Mackenzie (*anxious*) Mr Paterson.

Paterson (*ignoring* **Mackenzie**) Oh, we should have some soup, should we not?

Innkeeper We do a very fine lambshead broth.

Paterson Lambshead broth? Hmmmm . . . let us have something finer. Something . . . grander.

Innkeeper   Pottage of venison?

Paterson   Very good. Pottage of venison. Two large tureens.

Innkeeper   Two large tureens . . . pottage . . . of venison. Were you aware, Mr Paterson, that the Ship Tavern is renowned for its eel and oyster pie?

Paterson   Is it now? Then we shall have the Ship Tavern's eel and oyster pie. And plenty of it.

Innkeeper   Eel and oyster pie . . .

Paterson   And two ducks.

Innkeeper   Two ducks.

Paterson   Two ducks. Is that enough? Make that three ducks!

Innkeeper   Three ducks.

Paterson   And five chickens with gooseberries.

Innkeeper (*now struggling to keep up*)   Five chickens with goose –

Mackenzie   I hope you're aware of the price of chickens, Mr Paterson?

Paterson (*to* **Innkeeper**)   Should we not also have some veal collops. Yes, why not? Veal collops, lots of veal collops.

Innkeeper   A few . . . pounds of veal collops?

Paterson   Very good. With a plate or two of sparagrass.

Innkeeper   Veal collops, sparagrass . . .

Paterson   A sleeve of mutton.

Innkeeper   Sleeve of –

Paterson   Mutton.

Innkeeper (*flustered*)   Mutton. Sleeve of mutton.

Paterson   And two dozen bottles of your very finest claret.

Mackenzie (*shocked*)   Mr Paterson!

Innkeeper   Finest claret . . .

Paterson   Then we will want fruit, cheeses, bread, ale, brandy.

Innkeeper   Fruit . . . cheeses . . .

Paterson   French brandy.

Innkeeper   French, of course, Mr Paterson, for you, sir.

Mackenzie   This will cost a large sum of money, Mr Paterson.

Paterson   I think that will be all. Oh. Tobacco and pipes.

Innkeeper   Tobacco . . . and pipes . . .

Paterson   If you excel yourself, you will be well rewarded. And a shilling each for the serving boys. If they do not spill the soup. Come along Mackenzie.

Paterson *heads towards the door.* **Mackenzie** *follows, shaking his head.*

Innkeeper   Yes, Mr Paterson. Thank you, Mr Paterson. We look forward to receiving you and your guests.

Paterson   Yes, yes. Goodbye. (*Makes to leave.*)

Innkeeper   Oh, Mr Paterson, sorry. I nearly forgot. Number of guests. We can accommodate up to forty. How many will you be?

Paterson   Six.

Innkeeper   Six?

Paterson   Aye. Six.

Innkeeper   Six?

Paterson   Aye. Six.

Innkeeper   Of course, we're grateful for your business, Mr Paterson. But . . . are you quite sure? I mean, all that food and drink for . . . six.

Paterson I am quite sure.

Innkeeper Well . . . those must be mighty hungry men, Mr Paterson. And mighty thirsty.

Paterson They are, sir, they are. They're Members of Parliament.

Paterson *and* **Mackenzie** *leave.*

The **Nameless Of The Earth** *climb down onto the stage, singing. The* **Innkeeper** *shucks off his outer clothing, revealing the same rags as the* **Nameless**, *whom he joins.*

Song No. 1 The Nameless of the Earth

Nameless *It must be nice*
So nice
Nice to have the money
To order up a duck
Or chicken
Or veal.
To sit down to a meal
And have enough to eat
Oh what a treat
To have enough to eat.

Clothes stands are rolled on with articles of **MPs'** *clothing, which they put on. Two of the* **Nameless** *adopt the dress of* **Serving Maids** *while one dresses as a* **Serving Boy.**

Nameless *All history is written by the winners*
No place for us poor sinners
Unknown
Unsung
The nameless of the earth.
Despised, forgotten,
Of humble birth
Of little worth.
Although
We know
That history is written by the winners
We never give up hope

The nameless of the earth
All live in hope.

First Nameless   *So let us have a play*
In which the nameless of the earth
Will have a role.

Second Nameless   *A little play encompassing*
Each immortal soul.

Paterson *enters.*

Third Nameless   *And here's the lovely actor*
Who agreed to play the lead

Fourth Nameless   *Oh yes, I like the look of him*

Fifth Nameless   *He's exactly what we need.*

Food is laid out.

Nameless   *Aye, every now and then*
The nameless of the earth can still be heard
Can dream at least
Of one day being invited to the feast.

Scene Two – The Ship Tavern, Edinburgh

Five of the **Nameless** *are now* **MPs***, rather aware of their own importance. As they take their seats at table* **Paterson** *enters. The* **Serving Boy** *stands discreetly to one side.*

Paterson   Gentlemen. Welcome. What a pleasure it is to have your company. Your . . . esteemed company.

There is a murmur of satisfaction. The **Serving Maids** *withdraw.*

Paterson   I know you are dedicated men. I know how hard you work on Scotland's behalf. And I know it can't be easy, sitting up there in Parliament Hall day in day out listening to the endless blather of the Scottish aristocracy – those perfumed peacocks who neither see nor sense the tide of history.

They nod and smile, recognising the picture.

First MP   True enough, true enough.

Paterson   They resent you, gentlemen. Like you they may be members of Parliament, but they are the past, and you are the future. *We* are the future. Men who understand the meaning of money. Men who can do so much for this nation. If only we're allowed to change the old way of doing things.

Second MP   I never realised that Scotland was so close to your heart, Mr Paterson.

Third MP   Aye, you've spent a great part of your life abroad, have you not?

Second MP (*citing a heinous offence*)   Much of it in England.

Paterson   Should a man be blamed for leaving his native land in the hope of making his fortune?

Second MP   No, but –

Paterson   You think I could have founded the Bank of England without ever leaving Scotland, do you?

First MP   No need to boast, Mr Paterson. We all know how important you are. We just wonder why you've left behind all your fashionable friends in London in order to come back and scheme and plot amidst the stinking streets of Edinburgh.

Paterson   Because my country needs me. What has Scotland presently got to offer the world? Go on, gentlemen. Tell me.

Underscoring ends. **Paterson** *looks at the* **MPs** *challengingly. For a few moments there is silence around the table.*

Fourth MP   Fish.

Paterson   Fish?!

Fourth MP   Aye. It is my belief that the abundance of fish in Scotland is divine compensation for the lack of sunshine.

Paterson   Very well. Fish. What else?

The two **Serving Maids** *leave.*

Fifth MP   Hides.

Third MP   Coal.

First MP   Salt.

Fourth MP   Whisky.

Second MP   And knitted hosiery. We sell to England prodigious quantities of knitted hosiery.

Paterson   Oh, damn your knitted hosiery, sir. Scotland will not become great through the exporting of socks. A few rickety carts trundling down to England loaded with knitting is not going to do much for us. The advancement of overseas trade. That is what'll save Scotland from its present miserable condition.

Fourth MP   It is not so easy. Other countries will not permit us to trade with their colonies.

Paterson   Then Scotland must have colonies of its own.

Second MP (*laughs*)   You were a aye a bit of a dreamer, Mr Paterson.

Paterson   We all dream, do we not? It's what you do with your dream, that's what matters.

First MP (*dismissively*)   Yes, but the idea of a Scottish, colony . . . really, sir . . .

Paterson   The English have colonies. The Spanish have colonies. The French have colonies. The Portuguese have colonies. The Dutch have colonies. Even Denmark has colonies. Why should not Scotland have its colonies?

Third MP   Because Scotland's too poor. And too small. Do you mean to tell me that a nation of a million souls can conquer the globe?

Paterson   It's not conquest that I have in mind, sir. It is trade. Trade. The great civilising force of the future. And in a few days' time you'll have your chance to vote for the bill that will make it all possible.

Fourth MP   Oh, you want our votes, eh? I thought maybe you did. (*Looks at others, chuckles knowingly.*)

Paterson   I do. Yes, I do. Listen. Why has England been so successful in overseas trade? Because of the East India Company – and all the powers that have been given it by the English Parliament. Now it's our turn to do the same. When the Bill comes before you next week, I ask you to vote to establish Scotland's very own joint stock trading company. The Company of Scotland. Financed by private investment, protected by the state. Give this company powers. Grant it monopolies. Free it from the burden of taxation.

First MP   And will your new company stop the harvests from failing? (*Takes a big mouthful of food.*) Three years in a row we've had famine. Failed harvest after failed harvest.

The **Serving Maids** *enter with more food.*

Paterson   If we had the wealth, we could import food. And what now offers the fastest, most certain path to wealth? The joint stock company. There's no greater instrument for creating wealth. It's the most ingenious of all modern inventions.

First MP   To my mind, when there's a sudden fashion for new financial instruments, it is time to close your purse. There's aye some clever fellow who claims he's found a new road to riches. Some of us would prefer to risk our money in a more pleasurable manner.

Fifth MP   Like a wee game of cards.

First MP   Like a wee game of cards.

Paterson   Ah, but I can take away risk.

First MP   How would you do that?

Paterson   In the past, a man would invest in one ship going on one voyage. If that ship failed to return, he would lose everything. Now the risk is spread . . . you are not investing in a single voyage. You're investing in a company. A joint stock company set up by Parliament itself. A company that's as powerful as the nation itself. A company with its own ships. A company with its own colonies.

Fifth MP (*warming to the idea*)   A Scottish colony. 'Tis a bold idea.

Second MP   It may be worth . . . considering.

First MP   Aye, after all, Paterson, we're men of the world. We're not against earning the odd shilling.

Paterson   Yes, and when the sands of history are shifting, that's when a man of the world can make a fortune. And at the same time, benefit his native land. Wealth for one. Wealth for all, that's what I'm offering. We are entering a new age. Men will trade not only in goods but in company shares. Buying and selling. Selling and buying. Making money out of money. Trade will increase trade. Money will beget money. This is the simple idea that is going to transform the world. What I offer you, gentlemen, is nothing less than wealth without end.

There is a moment's silence. The **MPs** *accept* **Paterson**'s *ideas, tentatively at first.*

Song No. 2   Trade Begets Trade

First MP   *Trade begets trade . . . .*

Fourth MP   *Money makes money . . .*

Third MP   *Wealth creates wealth*

Second MP   *Riches from riches*

Fifth MP   *Piled upon riches*

First MP   *To the end of the world.*

They embrace the idea.

All MPs   *Trade begets trade*
Money makes money
Wealth creates wealth
Riches from riches
Piled upon riches
To the end of the world.

First MP   I am with you, Mr Paterson.

Third MP   So am I. A man needs to move with the times. You can be assured I will vote for the Bill. Scotland will have its trading company!

Second MP   I will speak to the motion.

First MP   Aye, it'll need some fine speech-making if we're to win the debate.

The other **MPs** *murmur their agreement.*

Paterson (*thoughtfully*)   I've been thinking . . . a debate. Do we really need a debate? Do we want some wheezing and decrepit old aristocrats telling Parliament that a joint stock company is not in their interests?

Fourth MP   The King would expect there to be a debate.

Paterson   The King is four hundred miles away.

Second MP (*shakes his head in disapproval*)   Aye, we have an absentee monarchy in this country.

Paterson   Isn't that the best kind? Especially with our own Parliament just up the road?

Fifth MP   I suppose . . . I mean, if the king's attention were elsewhere at the time.

Paterson   The King's attention is forever elsewhere. Yon Dutchman has never even set foot in Scotland, why should he start now? No, the King will leave everything to Tweedale, as he always does. Do not trouble yourselves with a debate, gentlemen. Be bold. Be brave. Be the messengers of a new world.

The music returns, now in a mood of religious fervour.

All MPs   *Trade begets trade*
Money makes money
Wealth creates wealth
Riches from riches
Piled upon riches
To the end of the world.

A splendidly dressed **Tweedale** *is flown in (or enters). The* **MPs**
leave. **Paterson** *leaves or goes to the side of the stage and observes.*

Scene Three – Parliament Hall, Edinburgh

A Sergeant of Arms *enters, bearing a sceptre. Lose music.*

Sergeant   This session of the Parliament of Scotland is
hereby holden and begun at Edinburgh upon this the
twenty-sixth day of June, one thousand, six hundred and
ninety five, presided over by his grace the Marquis of
Tweedale, Lord High Chancellor of Scotland.

Tweedale *looks around a little confused. The* **Sergeant** *looks up,
whistles or signals, and a parliamentary Bill flies in, festooned with
seals and ribbons.* **Tweedale** *reads from it.*

Tweedale (*reads*)   His Majesty understanding that several
persons are willing to engage themselves with great sums of
money in a trade to be exercised from this Kingdom, does
hereby grant unto them a monopoly on trade to Asia, Africa
and America, together with exemption from all taxation for
a period of twenty-one years.

MPs (*off or recorded*)   Hear! Hear!

Tweedale   The said persons shall form a joint stock
trading company, which shall be known as the Company of
Scotland.

MPs (*off or recorded*)   Hear! Hear!

Tweedale   This Company is hereby empowered to equip, fit, set out and navigate ships from any of the ports and places of this Kingdom, in warlike or in other manner to any Lands, Islands, Countries or places in Asia, Africa, or America, and there to plant colonies and build Cities, Towns and Forts.

MPs (*off or recorded*)   Hear! Hear! Hear!

Tweedale   The passing into law of this Bill shall be accompanied by the creation of a Scottish bank in whom all men may place their trust. The directors of this new Company shall be those named in the Bill.

MPs (*off or recorded*)   Hear! Hear! Hear!

Tweedale *snaps his fingers.*

Tweedale (*peevishly*)   Sceptre!

He touches the Bill with the sceptre.

Sergeant   The Bill is touched with the royal sceptre and becomes law.

*The **Nameless** change clothes to become directors of the Company of Scotland. **Tweedale** hands the sceptre back. A few bars of music are heard as **Tweedale** flies out or leaves.*

Scene Four – Paterson's office, Edinburgh

Mackenzie *enters, carrying a ledger, places it on a high desk or table or lectern and prepares to write.* **Balfour** *and* **Blackwood** *enter, each with a glass of red wine in his hand.*

Balfour   Here's tae us, wha's like us, gey few and they're aw deid!

Blackwood   Aye, it's time to celebrate all right.

Balfour   Scotland! Scotland will conquer the globe!

Mackenzie (*coughs to attract their attention*)   Gentleman, Roderick Mackenzie at your service. If you would kindly sign the Company articles (*holds out quill*).

Balfour   Aye, all in good time, sir, all in good time. (*Raises his glass to* **Blackwood**.) To the Company of Scotland!

Blackwood   The Company of Scotland!

Mackenzie   Each director of the company is required to sign the articles.

Balfour   Oh, very well, very well.

Mackenzie   Here, please. Just below Mr Paterson's name. (*Signs.*)

Mackenzie   Thank you, Mr Balfour. (*Gives quill to* **Blackwood**.)

Blackwood   Is it my signature you want?

Mackenzie (*wondering at the stupidity*)   Yes.

Blackwood   Here?

Mackenzie (*with forced patience*)   Yes.

Blackwood *signs.*

Mackenzie   Thank you, Mr Blackwood.

Erskine *enters.*

Balfour   Mr Erskine. Will you join us in a glass?

Erskine   A small one. I am here to sign the articles, not carouse late into the night. (*Signs.*)

Borland (*entering*)   I am glad to hear it. (*Signs.*) You will have a glass of water for me, I hope?

Blackwood (*puzzled*)   A glass of water?

Balfour (*pouring another glass of wine*)   Scotland! Scotland will rule the world.

Mackenzie (*without looking up from ledger*)   Do you think that's maybe a wee bit ambitious, Mr Balfour?

Balfour   Aye well, let's rule bits of it.

Erskine   Which bits? That's the question, is it not?

Balfour   Big bits.

Paterson (*enters*)   Gentleman, it is time to make plans.

Erskine   Good. Here we are, directors of this new company of yours, Paterson, and we don't even know where you plan to establish the first colony.

Blackwood   It'll be somewhere overseas.

All *turn and look for a moment, wondering whether* **Blackwood** *is as stupid as that sounded.*

Erskine (*to* **Paterson**)   We're thinking of the East Indies, are we not?

Balfour   Aye, the East Indies, that's where we should be heading. Or Africa. Or the Caribbean. Or all three!

Erskine (*to* **Paterson**)   The Act has been passed. Now's the time to decide where we trade, where we plant our first colony.

Paterson   All in good time, Mr Erskine. There are ships to be built. Men to be hired. Supplies to be bought. All this will require a great deal of money. Most of it will have to come from English investors.

Blackwood   English investors, that's a good idea. It will require a journey to England.

Erskine   I believe that's generally where the English are to be found, Mr Blackwood.

Paterson   London will be the foundation of this endeavour. It's there I intend to start.

Blackwood   Oh, it's a grand place, London.

Balfour   Only because it's full of Scots. (*Pours himself another glass.*)

Erskine (*to* **Paterson**)   You will have a target sum in mind?

Paterson   Yes.

Erskine   And . . . ?

Balfour (*thinking he's being ambitious*)   I suggest you aim at raising one hundred thousand pounds.

Paterson   I will raise more than that.

Balfour   That's the spirit, sir! Two hundred thousand!

Paterson   More than two hundred thousand.

Balfour   Yes! You're a great man, Mr Paterson. May the good Lord bless you and the Company of Scotland.

Erskine (*coldly, to* **Paterson**)   So how much do you have in mind?

Paterson   Three hundred thousand.

Balfour (*triumphantly*)   Three hundred thousand!

Mackenzie (*looks up sharply*)   Three hundred thousand?

Paterson   I want us to build a trading fleet that'll be the envy of the world. Not those sorry excuses for ships that Scotland presently possesses. I mean great ships, mighty ships, as mighty as those of the Dutch. Ships that will be looked on with awe. Ships that speak of wealth. Ships that make a man's heart race. Ships that will have men rushing to invest. We'll open a subscription book in London. It will not take long to raise what we need. The money always follows the money.

A **Servant Boy** *and* **Girl** *prepare* **Paterson** *for the journey.*

Mackenzie   It will have to be carefully accounted for, Mr Paterson. There must be no irregularities. We have Scotland's reputation to protect. Every last penny must be recorded in these ledgers.

Paterson (*laughs*)   Oh, Mackenzie, Mackenzie. It is good we have made you our Company Secretary. It will let you give full rein to your anxiety. Every Company needs a man who worries about the detail.

Erskine   The English will rush to invest in a Scottish Company trading overseas, will they? They will trust us?

Blackwood   They will certainly trust Mr Paterson. Everyone trusts Mr Paterson.

Erskine   Let us hope so.

Blackwood   The man who founded the Bank of England? I don't think there is any doubt upon the matter. How could they not put their money in the hands of a man who once ran a bank?

Balfour   Very good point, Mr Blackwood, very good point.

Erskine   You do not think the English merchants will see us as a threat?

Paterson   They may. Or as an investment. Never underestimate the lure of an investment, Mr Erskine. (*To* **Mackenzie**.) Well, don't just stand there, man, you and I are leaving for London.

Paterson *leaves.* **Balfour** *and* **Blackwood** *perform a skippy little dance and reprise the previous number, this time in a skittish version.*

Song No. 3   Trade Begets Trade (Reprise)

Balfour & Blackwood   *Trade begets trade*
Money makes money
Wealth creates wealth
Riches from riches
Piled upon riches
To the end of the world.

Balfour *and* **Blackwood** *dance off in the opposite direction from* **Paterson**. **Mackenzie** *readies himself for the journey.*

Erskine   He plays his cards close to his chest, that man.

Mackenzie   Mr Paterson knows what he's doing.

Erskine   He has no doubt told you about where we are to found our colony?

Mackenzie   No.

Erskine   Really?

Mackenzie   I said no, Mr Erskine.

Erskine   This secrecy. What is the purpose of it?

Mackenzie   If it were to become public knowledge, other nations might send their ships there before us.

Erskine   He doesn't trust us to hold our tongues?

Mackenzie   Why should he?

Erskine   There must be trust. I don't do business with men I don't trust.

Mackenzie   Then you must do gey little business, Mr Erskine.

Erskine   What if he doesn't know? What if that's his secret? That he doesn't even know where this colony is to be?

Mackenzie   Och, now you're being silly, Mr Erskine. *(Turns.)* Mr Paterson! Wait for me!

Mackenzie *hurries off after* **Paterson**. **Erskine** *leaves*.

Scene Five – the Streets of London (alternatively a coffee house)

A dance routine. **Investors** *thrust / throw banknotes at* **Paterson**, *while* **Mackenzie** *nervously collects the stray notes. While this is happening,* **Three Nameless** *enter downstage and sing.*

Song No. 4   When You've Founded A Bank

First Nameless   *Regardless of rank*
When you've founded a bank
Society opens its doors
And those in high places
with big smiling faces
Are suddenly down on all fours.

Second Nameless   *Though your mind may be blank*
Once you've founded a bank
It's like leading a lamb to the slaughter.
Old men in fine breeches
Will make lovely speeches
And leave you alone with their daughter.

Third Nameless   *Now let us be frank*
When you've founded a bank
Society pays you attention
You are keenly awaited
And greeted and feted
And end up with quite a nice pension.

They all three do a little dance. **King William** *enters, dressed for hunting. He lingers upstage while* **Joost***, a handsome young courtier enters, carrying a cushion with rings and jewellery. He goes over to observe* **Paterson***. The dance ends. The* **Nameless** *leave.* **Paterson** *is left breathlessly scrambling around stuffing banknotes into his pockets.* **Joost** *stares at this undignified scene for a moment or two.*

Joost (*disdainfully*)   The King commands you to attend upon him.

Paterson *dusts himself down, straightens his clothing.* **Mackenzie** *leaves.*

Scene Six – the Court of King William, London

King William *examines himself in the long mirror, coughs, fusses, examines his hunting outfit.*

Joost   Your Majesty. Mr William Paterson.

William *coughs again, ignores* **Paterson***, fusses with his clothing. He takes a ring, tries it on, discards it.* **Joost** *offers him another choice.*

William (*without turning round*)   I'm about to go hunting.

Paterson (*bows slightly*)   Your Majesty.

William   I do so love hunting. Do you hunt much yourself, Paterson?

Paterson   Hunting is not something in which I indulge, Sire.

William   How very odd. (*He and* **Joost** *exchange glances in confirmation of the oddity.*) And life in Scotland? Is it bearable?

Paterson   It suits me well enough, Sire.

William   I have never been to Scotland. Tell me, is it true that to avoid the lice a gentleman must go to bed wearing gloves and stockings? (*Exchanges exaggerated looks of horror with* **Joost**.)

Paterson   That is to overstate the case.

William   Still, you must miss the pleasures of London life.

Paterson   I am happy to live in Scotland for the foreseeable future. A man has an attachment to the land of his birth.

William   And the purpose of your visit to England?

Paterson   I believe your Majesty is apprised of the purpose of my visit.

William (*his mood no longer playful*)   Yes. You are absolutely right. We are. You have opened subscription books here in London for this new Scotch Trading Company. And you have already raised three hundred thousand pounds. In just two weeks.

Paterson   In twelve days. To be precise. Sire.

William   Such a large sum in such a short time. Our men of wealth must love you very dearly.

Paterson   They trust me, Sire. I have experience in raising capital for new enterprises. The Bank of England. The Hampstead Water Company. The Southwark Corporation for the supply of –

William   Yes, that's the problem. You make people believe in you. We do not like it. You have a persuasive tongue.

We have nothing against your tongue, sir. It is a most accomplished instrument. You may do with your tongue what you will.

Joost *giggles.*

William (*contd.*)   Unless your tongue begins to damage English trading interests.

Paterson   I can assure your Majesty that –

William   The shareholders of the East India Company are unhappy. They do not want to see English wealth draining away to Edinburgh. And we certainly don't wish to see Scottish colonies set up in competition to English colonies. I want no distractions from the war with France. I have been ill served in Scotland. That old fool Tweedale exceeded his powers. This is what happens when I don't personally take command. I should go there myself. But I do not want to go to Scotland. It does not appeal. The weather. The filth. The drink.

Paterson   Your subjects in Scotland would be greatly heartened were Your Majesty pleased to go there.

William   I have sufficient problems at home. No King should have two Parliaments. One is more than enough. Two parliaments and one king. Two independent nations under one crown. Only the people of these islands could have devised such a regrettable constitutional settlement. Sooner or later there must be union between England and Scotland. It is obvious.

Paterson   The people of Scotland cling fiercely to their independence.

William   But I will not permit them to damage English trade. And I think the English Parliament is likely to feel the same. And now I am going hunting. Come along, Joost. (*Leaves.*)

Joost (*as he passes*)   Lik mijn reet.

Paterson   What?

Joost   Lik mijn reet.

Paterson   Sorry, I don't speak Dutch.

Joost   How very fortunate for you. (*Leaves.*)

Scene Seven – a London street or square

Paterson *alone on stage. A* **Town Crier** *enters, ringing a handbell. Behind him comes a* **Liveried Flunkey** *pushing a wooden wheelbarrow. As the* **Town Crier** *speaks,* **Paterson** *reluctantly empties his pockets of money into the wheelbarrow. Near the end, the* **Flunkey** *points at a pocket and* **Paterson** *takes out the last few notes he has missed.*

Town Crier   Hear ye! Hear ye! Hear ye! It is hereby solemnly resolved by the Sovereign Parliament of England and Ireland that the Directors of the Company of Scotland by raising monies in England under pretext of a Scotch Act of Parliament are guilty of a High Crime and Misdemeanour. It is further resolved that a Committee be appointed to prepare the impeachment of Mr William Paterson. (*Leaves. Off.*) Hear ye! Hear ye! Hear ye!

The **Servant** *with the wheelbarrow also leaves.*

Mackenzie (*entering*)   So, our Company is attacked in its swaddling clothes and strangled in its infancy.

Paterson   No.

He clicks his fingers and a **Servant** *enters with a trunk.*

Mackenzie   But they will impeach you.

Paterson   They threaten to. But that's only to frighten off the investors.

Mackenzie   It has succeeded. All the monies pledged have been withdrawn. We have raised not one penny. The investors are terrified.

Paterson   The English investors are terrified.

Mackenzie (*looks at trunk*)   You leave for Scotland?

Paterson   No. I leave for Amsterdam. And Rotterdam. And Hamburg. And Bremen. And Lübeck. The English are not the only people on this earth with money to invest.

Mackenzie   But . . . I mean . . . King William . . . . . He will hear of it. He will not like it. He has diverse interests. Interests and influence.

Paterson   Yes. But money also has influence.

Music.

Servant (*to audience*)   We will now pander to popular prejudice by offering a short and faintly anachronistic scene in which a number of foreigners are caricatured in an unacceptable manner. Any members of the audience who find this offensive may ask for their money back. Though they will not get it. Thank you. (*Picks up trunk and leaves.*)

Scene Eight – the capitals of Northern Europe

A few bars of appropriate national music announce each caricature as he opens a window or emerges through a door. The **French Merchant** *has a beret and a baguette, the* **German Merchant** *has sausages and wears Lederhosen, the* **Dutch Merchant** *wears clogs, carries tulips, and is perhaps dressed as a windmill, the* **Danish Merchant** *is dressed as a Viking. They dance and sing.*

Song No. 5   The International Language

Paterson   *Everybody speaks the language of money*
            It's the international language.
            And that's why we all get on

Foreign Merchants   *Jawohl.*
Bien sur.
Ja.
Jawel.

Paterson   *Everybody speaks the language of money,*
That's why we all get on.

Foreign Merchants   *That's why we all get on.*

Paterson   *Oh yes, that's why we all get on.*

Foreign Merchants   *That's why we all get on.*
Oh my, how we all get on.

They dance. Music changes or suddenly ceases as **Joost** *enters.*

Joost   King William has been informed that representatives of a Scotch trading Company are travelling the Continent endeavouring to raise money. (*The merchants put on an act of baffled innocence.*) His Majesty has commanded me most expressly to notify Your Magnificences that if you enter into business with these men his Majesty will regard it as an affront to his royal authority and (*heavily*) he will not fail to resent it. (*Leaves.*)

There is a clap of thunder and they gasp in fear. The **Foreign Merchants** *go to* **Mackenzie** *and take back their bags of coins.*

Merchants   Sorry!

They slam shut the doors or windows.

Paterson *stands there head bowed as* **Mackenzie** *looks on anxiously.*

Mackenzie   Let's go home, Mr Paterson.

He does not reply.

Mackenzie   All doors are closed against us. The King will never allow Scotland to have its colonies. It was a noble dream, Mr Paterson, but that's all it is now. A dream.

Blackout.

Scene Nine – a room in Paterson's house, Edinburgh

It is comfortable but restrained. In one corner a large globe of the world. **Mrs Paterson** *is directing* **Two Male Servants** *who are carrying in a piece of furniture covered by a cloth. A* **Servant Girl** *is standing watching.*

Mrs Paterson   Over there.

The **Servants** *place the piece of furniture where she indicates. They remove the cloth. It is a brand new day bed. She steps back to consider it.*

Mrs Paterson   A wee bit more to the left. (*Pause.*) No, more to the right. (*Pause.*) No, back where it was. Yes. That'll do it.

The **Servants** *make to leave.*

Mrs Paterson   It doesn't look right.

The **Servants** *go back to the day bed.*

Mrs Paterson   Ach no, it's fine. Leave it where it is. It just needs the new cushions.

The **Domestic Servants** *withdraw.*

Mrs Paterson   Well where are they, then? Where are the new cushions? Come along, lassie, don't just stand there looking glaekit.

Servant Girl   Sorry, Mrs Paterson. They're in yon kist.

Mrs Paterson   Bring them here, then.

Servant Girl   Yes, Madam.

Mrs Paterson   And will you stop calling it a kist? It's not some farmworker's box for storing oats. It's a French linenfold coffer. In walnut.

Servant Girl   Yes, Madam. (*Takes out the brightly coloured cushions, unwrapping them from paper.*) Oh, they're so bonnie.

Mrs Paterson *points at the day bed. The* **Servant Girl** *places the cushions on the day bed.* **Mrs Paterson** *assesses them. They make a bold splash of colour in an otherwise dark and simple room.*

Off: Dogs bark. Rattle of a carriage. Horses neigh. Male voices shouting orders.

Servant Girl   The maister! The maister is hame! I will go help.

Mrs Paterson   Go on then!

The **Servant Girl** *leaves.* **Mrs Paterson** *hurriedly checks her appearance in the mirror.*

She goes back to the cushions, rearranges them to her satisfaction. **Paterson** *enters purposefully, carrying a leather satchel.*

Mrs Paterson   Will . . .

He crosses to her, picks her up, whirls her round, kisses her.

Mrs Paterson   So, it went well?

Paterson   No. It went badly.

Mrs Paterson   So why then are you so cheerful?

Paterson   Aha, that is for you to guess. (*Looks at the day bed.*) What in the name of God is that?

Mrs Paterson   It's a reposing bed.

Paterson   A what?!

Mrs Paterson   A reposing bed. For a rest during the day. Look. It has straps here. So you can adjust it. It's all the rage.

Paterson   Hmmm . . . To my mind, a bed is for sleeping in at night. Among other purposes.

Mrs Paterson   But I bought it for you.

Paterson   I don't want it. (*Realises he's being too harsh.*) Sorry. I mean, it looks very nice. By all means let's keep it. (*He takes out a manuscript from his satchel.*) But at this moment I have reading to do.

Mrs Paterson Will you not rest after the journey?

Paterson No. I cannot.

She takes the manuscript, looks at it. He tries to take it away from her. She dodges him, walks away and reads it out.

Mrs Paterson (*reads*) A new Voyage and Description of the Isthmus of America, giving an account of the Author's abode there . . .

Paterson Give it to me. Please.

Mrs Paterson (*Dodges away from him and reads.*) . . . the form and make of the country, the Coasts, Hills, Rivers, Beasts, Birds, and Fish . . .

Paterson I will thank you to –

Mrs Paterson (*reads*) The Indian Inhabitants. Their Features, their Customs, their Language. With remarkable Occurences in the South Sea and Elsewhere. By . . . Lionel Wafer.

He tries to take it away from her. They are now in a sort of embrace. She teases him, holding the manuscript out of reach.

Mrs Paterson And who is this Lionel Wafer? It's a damned strange name for a man.

Paterson He is a surgeon. A sailor. A traveller in Central America. This is his journal. Not yet published. I will finish reading it tonight.

Mrs Paterson Must it be tonight?

Paterson Yes.

Mrs Paterson Judging by your mood, you raised all the money.

Paterson I did not raise any money. The King has blocked us at every turn. The money will have to be raised in Scotland. In its entirety.

Mrs Paterson   Is that possible?

Paterson   Aye. If I can but light a flame that will burn in the heart of every Scot from the Borders to the Orkneys.

Mrs Paterson   And can you?

Paterson   I believe I can. With God's help. And perhaps a little help from Mr Wafer.

She looks at him, she looks at the manuscript, she looks back at him. It dawns on her.

Mrs Paterson (*with growing excitement*)   Will . . . ? . . . Is this where you are to found your colony? . . . It is, isn't it? This is where you plan to found your colony.

Paterson   Give me back the manuscript!

Mrs Paterson   Is it?!

Paterson   Yes. (*Pause.*) On all of God's earth, I cannot imagine a more propitious place. The manuscript. Please. I cannot sleep till I've read it to the end.

She hands it back to him.

Mrs Paterson   Then you must read it to the end. Goodnight, Will.

She kisses him and withdraws. She gets to the door, turns, waits. He is already staring at the manuscript. He looks up.

Paterson   Oh. Sorry. Goodnight.

Mrs Paterson   Goodnight.

She leaves.

Underscoring.

Paterson *lays out the manuscript on a desk or table. He picks up a few pages, paces, reads. He crosses to the big globe, spins it gently. He puts a finger on it and it stops turning.*

Scene Ten – the Offices of the Company of Scotland

Paterson *remains where he was as the scene transforms into a meeting room in Edinburgh. Three of the* **Nameless** *are getting dressed up while a long wooden table with quills and pens is set up, with a row of seven chairs behind it. The Coat of Arms of the Company of Scotland flies in.*

Underscoring continues.

First Nameless   Who are we now?

Second Nameless   I think we're on the board of directors.

First Nameless   Is that right?

Third Nameless   Aye. We're directors of the Company of Scotland. We get to decide everything.

First Nameless   But I don't know anything.

Third Nameless   That doesn't matter.

First Nameless   Do we get paid?

Third Nameless   Oh aye.

They are finally dressed as **Directors** *and are joined by* **Balfour**, **Blackwood**, **Erskine** *and the* **Rev. Francis Borland**, *a Church of Scotland Minister. To one side a* **Servant** *hovers discreetly. The* **Directors** *solemnly take their seats.* **Paterson** *makes his pitch.*

Paterson   Gentlemen. I can reveal where our colony is to be founded.

There is a murmur of anticipation.

Paterson   I propose that we send a fleet to Central America. A Scottish expedition to occupy the Gulf of Darien. (*Pointing at globe.*) Here. The narrowest part of the isthmus of Panama that links North and South America. On one side, the Atlantic. On the other, the Pacific. Two great oceans separated by one tiny neck of land. Across this tiny neck of land we build a trading road. Linking the two oceans. At a stroke, the whole shape of world trade is transformed. The journey to Asia is halved. The time and expense of navigation to China – halved. To Japan – halved. To the Spice Islands – halved. The sale of European goods – doubled. And for every journey across that isthmus the merchants of the world will pay us a levy . . . Scotland will control the flow of commodities from east to west. And from west to east. We will be the proprietors of this land called Darien. We shall give laws unto both oceans. We shall be the arbitrators of the commercial world.

Lose music. A silence descends.

Erskine   Mr Paterson. This is a vast undertaking.

Paterson   It is, Mr Erskine, it is.

Erskine   The Spaniard will not like it. The Dutch will not like it. The English will not like it.

Paterson   That is possible.

Erskine   We will need to build a mighty fleet. Well armed.

Paterson   Aye.

Balfour   It's a bold plan. A bonnie plan. I like it, Mr Paterson, I like it.

Erskine   It is an expensive plan. Impossibly expensive. We have scarce any funds.

Paterson   We will have. I promise you. We will have.

Erskine   How?

Borland   The Good Lord will provide.

Blackwood   Tell us more about the Gulf of . . . what's it called again?

Erskine (*irritated*)   Darien.

Blackwood   Yes. Darien. (*To neighbour.*) It's called Darien.

Erskine   Have you ever been there, Mr Paterson?

Paterson   As you know, Mr Erskine, I've voyaged extensively in the Americas.

Erskine   But not set foot in Darien itself.

Paterson   No.

Erskine   No, I thought not.

Paterson   But I've spoken to those who have. And I have documents. (*Handing them over.*) Letters. Affadavits. Reports from travellers. (*Lowers his voice to emphasise importance of confidentiality.*) Among them, this manuscript. Lent to me by the author in person. It must be read by nobody but yourselves. (*Hands over a manuscript.*)

The **Directors** *glance at the manuscript.* **Blackwood** *appropriates it.*

Erskine   Lionel . . . Wafer?

Paterson   Yes.

Erskine   It is somehow not a name that inspires confidence.

Blackwood   It says here (*Reads.*) 'The country I am going to describe is the narrowest part of the Isth . . . the Isth . . . the Isth-mus of America.' It's a bugger of a word that. Isth-mus.

Borland   Who is Lionel Wafer?

Paterson   A most respectable and reliable gentleman, who has visited Darien and knows it well. Would you like to meet him?

Blackwood   Is he here?

Paterson   Indeed. (*Nods to* **Servant**.)

The **Servant** *leaves.*

Blackwood (*to neighbour*)   He is here.

Erskine   You're full of tricks, Mr Paterson.

Servant (*enters*)   Mr Lionel Wafer.

Wafer *enters.* **Paterson** *shakes him by the hand.* **Erskine** *takes the manuscript and looks at it.*

Paterson   It is good of you to attend here today.

Wafer   Well, you said that if I came to Edinburgh you'd –

Paterson (*interrupting*)   Yes, yes. Now these gentlemen would like to know more about the land you call Darien.

Wafer   Gentlemen. I am at your service.

Balfour   Tell us everything. Everything. The landscape, the features of the place. Is it mountainous? Is it flat? Is it wooded?

Wafer   There are low mountains. Some wooded. Where the River Darien meets the sea there's a fine bay with deep water.

Paterson   It affords a good anchorage?

Wafer   It's a first class anchorage.

Erskine (*looking at manuscript*)   Now wait. Now just wait. (*Reads.*) 'The shore of the isth-

Blackwood   Isthmus. It's pronounced isth-mus.

Erskine (*irritated*)   Yes, thank you Mr Blackwood. 'The shore of the isthmus is partially drowned, swampy, mangrove land, where there is no going ashore but up to the middle in mud.'

Wafer   Some of the coast is like that.

Paterson   But much of it is not?

Wafer   Much of it is not.

Blackwood (*nods, turns to others*)   Much of it is not.

Borland   The land. Is it fruitful?

Wafer   Yes. The natives grow plantains in great abundance. There also grows a fruit called a banana.

Blackwood   A what?

Wafer   A banana.

All Directors (*in wonderment, to audience*)   A ba-na-na.

Borland   Do the natives consume strong liquor?

Wafer   They make a drink of fermented maize. They drink large quantities of it and are very fond of it. It makes them belch very much. And in their drink the men are very quarrelsome.

Blackwood   Tis the right place for a Scottish colony.

Balfour   The women. Tell us about the womenfolk, Mr Wafer.

Borland   Why? Why would you wish to know about the womenfolk?

Paterson (*to* **Wafer**)   I gather they wear no clothes?

Borland   What?

Wafer   Ordinarily, they wear no clothes.

Balfour   None at all?

Wafer   They have but a small piece of cloth . . . in front of their . . . in front. And tied behind with a thread.

There is a stirring of embarrassment and ill-concealed interest.

Blackwood   Is it a strong thread? (*To a neighbour.*) It'd have to be a strong thread.

Borland   There must be ministers on this expedition. To save our people from licentiousness.

Erskine   There may not be an expedition. It is most unlikely that money can be raised for such a venture. And why have others not built a trading road across the isthmus?

Blackwood (*to himself*)   Isth-mus. Isth-muss . . . Maybe I've got it wrong. Isthm-us . . .

Erskine   Will you be quiet, sir!

Borland   The relation between the sexes? Do they marry, or do they just . . . breed like dogs?

Blackwood *goes back to looking at the manuscript.*

Wafer   They marry. But the women are little better than slaves to their husbands. Though you would never know it, because they do their work so readily and cheerfully. They observe their husbands with a profound respect and duty upon all occasions.

Balfour   So their culture is quite advanced?

Erskine   I doubt that these travellers' tales are an adequate basis upon which to consider founding a colony. And if it is so wonderful why has it not been occupied by the Spaniard?

First Nameless (*as Councillor*)   Aye, why has it not been occupied by the Spaniard?

Second Nameless (*as Councillor*)   It's a very good question.

Blackwood (*looking up from manuscript*)   You know what's bothering me? What's bothering me is this: why has it not been occupied by the Spaniard?

All turn to give him a withering look.

Erskine   Will the Spanish take kindly to a rival colony set up in their midst?

Borland   We will drive them out. Those idolatrous Papish hordes shall be put to the sword.

Paterson   The Spanish are not in Darien itself. And if they do come at us, we will be well armed. We'll be prepared. Men will fight and die to defend our colony, because it is our future.

Erskine   Hmmmm . . . I cannot decide if your confidence be bluff, or truth, or simply a means of deceiving yourself.

Paterson *is for a moment on the back heel.* **Balfour** *takes the manuscript.*

Paterson   Mr Wafer has not yet spoken of the gold, have you, Mr Wafer?

Erskine   Gold?

Paterson   Gold.

All Directors (*turning like automatons to the audience*)   Gold!

Borland   There is gold in Darien?

Wafer   Yes. Mines of gold. And also in the rivers.

Balfour (*excited*)   Yes. Look. It says here, it says here . . . where is it? Yes . . . here. (*Reads.*) 'We passed by a river where men were gathering gold.'

Erskine   Gold . . .

All Directors (*to audience*)   Gold!

Balfour   So there is gold to be panned from the rivers? How wonderful, how marvellous. Gold in the rivers!

Paterson *has wandered over to the manuscript sheets, he picks one out, slides it over to* **Blackwood***, his finger on a paragraph.*

Wafer   Yes. In fact, one of the rivers in the South is called the Gold River.

Blackwood (*reading the part indicated*)   'Gold dust is washed down the rivers and gathered by the natives in great quantity.' You have witnessed this?

Wafer   Yes. The men use gold to make ornamentations for themselves.

Borland   So the men wear clothing?

Wafer   No.

Borland   How then do they wear ornamentations of gold?

Blackwood   In their hair, I expect. Wee gold clips in their hair, eh, am I right? Like lassies.

Wafer   No. The men fashion a vessel of gold, like the extinguisher of a candle, which they wear upon the penis, close to the pubes. They keep it there with a string going about their waists.

Erskine   Ye Gods.

Wafer   They leave the scrotum exposed, having no sense of shame with reference to that.

Blackwood   Must be awful in the winter. Do they have a winter?

Wafer   They have a rainy season.

Blackwood   Well, you wouldnae want to go out in the rain dressed like that, would you?

Borland   We must take the gospel to these poor wretches.

Paterson   I believe Mr Wafer has brought back with him an example . . .

Wafer   Yes. Yes, indeed.

He takes out a cloth, carefully unwraps it. Inside it is a solid gold penis gourd. He holds it up. It is surprisingly large.

Erskine   Oh, my heavens.

Balfour   It is . . . it is . . . it is . . .

Blackwood   Big.

Balfour   Gold.

Wafer   Yes. Solid gold.

It is passed around.

Erskine   Gentlemen. Please! Let us not get carried away. However alluring the prospects of a colony in Darien, we have no funds. (*Takes the penis gourd, hands it to* **Wafer**, *who wraps it up again.*) Mr Paterson, you have been to London, Hamburg, Amsterdam . . . And have raised how much for the Company?

Paterson   Next to nothing. No matter. We will raise the money in Scotland.

Erskine (*in disbelief*)   All of it?

Paterson   Aye. It can be done.

Erskine   Can it?

Paterson   It can be done if it is done at speed, so people have no time to discover doubt. Each man must fear that if he doesn't subscribe, he will lose forever the chance of great riches.

Balfour   That's how it worked with the Bank of England, is it not, Mr Paterson?

Paterson   Just so. In founding the Bank of England we allocated only six weeks from the opening of the books, and our funding was finished in nine days. You see, if a thing go not on with the first heat, the raising of a fund seldom succeeds.

Erskine   And why should that be?

Paterson   Because, Mr Erskine, the multitude are commonly led more by example than by reason.

Erskine   And you believe this is possible even though you failed to raise funds abroad?

Paterson   I didn't fail. The money was there. The English cheated Scotland of its due.

As **Paterson** *speaks, the* **Nameless of the Earth** *drift in, and his speech effectively becomes a speech to the audience / the people of Scotland. At some point, Saltires are brought in, perhaps paraded down through the audience and up on to the stage.*

Paterson   The English imagine we can do nothing without their help. But this is not true. Not if we believe in Scotland. Not if we believe in ourselves. Why should other countries have their colonies and not Scotland? Why should Scotland be left out? Are we more stupid than they? Less enterprising? Less ingenious? Less hard-working? I think not. It can be done. It can be done. (*Underscoring creeps in.*) This will be a national endeavour. A source of pride for every Scot. A promise of wealth for every subscriber. A promise of greatness for Scotland. Overnight this poor small nation will join the ranks of the rich and mighty. If we but act wisely and boldly, trade will increase trade, and money will beget money, and the trading world shall need no more to want work for their hands, but will rather want hands for their work. (*Pauses, then delivers his inspirational clincher.*) In Darien, gentlemen, I offer you the door of the seas and the keys of the universe.

Balfour, **Blackwood** *and* **Borland** *sing.* **Paterson** *goes over to* **Wafer** *and pays him off.* **Wafer** *leaves.*

Song No. 6   Let Scotland's Name

> *Let Scotland's name*
> *Across the world resound*
> *To foreign lands*
> *Where riches abound*
> *One pound today*
> *Tomorrow will be ten*
> *And Scotland will*
> *Be mighty once again.*

Erskine *takes* **Paterson** *to one side while* **Balfour**, **Blackwood** and **Borland** *and the other* **Directors** *leave.*

Erskine   I observe that Darien has become a wonderfully patriotic undertaking.

Paterson   I don't take your meaning, Mr Erskine.

Erskine   You're no nationalist, Mr Paterson. You're more at home in the drawing rooms of London, or Amsterdam or Berlin than you are in the coffee houses of Edinburgh. But to persuade the people to invest, you're waving the flag of St Andrew at them. How else are you going to raise these vast sums of money in a small poor country? I won't say I'm not impressed. You're a very persuasive man.

Paterson It is in the interests of the people of Scotland.

Erskine That's why you're doing it, is it? For the people of Scotland?

Paterson For myself and for the people of Scotland. Our interests are the same.

Erskine Are they?

Paterson History will prove me right.

Erskine Oh I'm not too interested in history. I'm interested in getting rich. Much the same as you are. But I know the risks. Do you think the people of Scotland know the risks?

Paterson Yes.

Erskine You've made it clear to them have you?

Paterson I can't offer certainty. Some things are in God's hands.

Erskine Oh yes. A great deal will be in God's hands. But no doubt you'll have had a word with him. A clever Scot aye gets the kirk on his side. (*Leaves.*)

Scene Eleven – a Protestant Church

Borland *steps up into the pulpit.*

Borland Galations Chapter Five Verse Seven: 'Be not deceived. God is not mocked. For whatever a man sows, that shall he also reap.' (*Fixes the congregation.*) I look around me and I see sin. I see sin and I see sinners. Aye, in this very congregation. I know you. The Lord knows you. He knows about your profaneness and your immorality, oh aye, he kens every detail. He sees your excessive drinking and your tippling and your fighting and your cursing. He hears you when you take the Lord's name in vain. He makes note of each abomination, and carefully enters the perpetrator's name in the ledger of eternal damnation. Whatever a man sows, that shall he also reap . . . . . But what if a man sows goodness, as the farmer sows his crops? So that there be not famine in the land? This nation has seen famine, like unto the great famine that was in the days of Abraham. When Isaac dwelt in the land of Gerar, and sowed in that land. But Isaac was blessed with a plentiful harvest. He received an hundredfold of what he had sown. And I believe that soon, the people of Scotland will receive an hundredfold for what they will sow. Aye, they will take their little wealth and see it grow, and the people of Scotland will wax great, as the nation waxes great. And the Lord will bless this nation and its great enterprise abroad and will bless all those who sow, for they shall reap. They shall reap an hundredfold.

Scene Twelve – the House of Mrs Purdie, High Street, Edinburgh

Mackenzie *enters as a tall stool and desk are set up on which is placed a large leather bound entry book.* **Mackenzie** *sits at it and keeps a record.* **Paterson** *enters and stands near him.*

Mackenzie   Edinburgh, the twentie sixth day of February, 1696. At the House of Mrs Purdie, in the North side of the High Street, over and against the Cross. (*Reads.*) Pursuant to an Act of Parliament, entitled Act for a Company Trading to Africa and the Indies, we, the under subscribers, do each of us become obleidged for the payment of the respective sums subscribed by us subject to the rules and constitutions of the said Company.

Ordinary Merchants *enter, stand around and seem reluctant to sign up.* **Mackenzie** *holds out the quill to them. No takers. He looks questioningly at* **Paterson**.

Mackenzie   Mr Paterson, you said –

Paterson   Shush.

Mackenzie   But we've been here nigh on an hour and nobody has yet –

Paterson   Patience, Mackenzie, patience.

Silence for a few seconds. Gasps from the crowd as the **Duchess of Hamilton** *enters.*

First Subscriber (*approaches the ledger and signs*)   Anne, Duchess of Hamilton and Chasterault. One thousand pounds.

Second Subscriber   Margarett, Countess of Rothesse. Two thousand pounds. (*Signs.*)

Third Subscriber   Lady Hope of Houpetoun. Three thousand pounds. (*Signs.*)

There is a growing sense of competition amongst the **Subscribers**.

First Subscriber (*coming back to the ledger*)   Anne, Duchess of Hamilton and Chasterault. For her son Murdoch, one thousand pounds.

Second Subscriber (*coming back to the ledger*)   Margarett, Countess of Rothesse. For her son Thomas, Earle of Haddington. Two thousand pounds. (*Signs.*)

Third Subscriber (*coming back to the ledger*)   Lady Hope of Hopetoun. For her nephew Hopetoun. Three thousand pounds. (*Signs.*)

Fourth Subscriber   David Lord Cardross. Five hundred pounds. (*Signs.*)

Fifth Subscriber   John Lord Glenorchy. Two thousand pounds. (*Signs.*)

Sixth Subscriber   James Byres, Merchant in Edinburgh. Two hundred pounds. (*Signs.*)

Paterson (*calmly*)   You see, my dear Mackenzie. The aristocracy still have their uses. Where the aristocracy go, others follow. God knows why, but they do. (*Smiles, bows as Duchess of Hamilton leaves.*) Your Grace.

Seventh Subscriber   Thomas Campbell, butcher in Edinburgh. Two hundred pounds.

Paterson   You see?

Paterson *continues to watch. Music. In a choreographed sequence the subscribers announce their investment to* **Mackenzie**.

One   Colin Campbell of Arkinlass. Five hundred pounds.

Two   John Swinton of that Ilk. One thousand pounds.

Three   Robert Douglas, Soap-Boiler in Leith. One hundred pounds.

Four   Andrew Broune, watchmaker in Edinburgh. Two hundred pounds.

Five   William Callender, merchant in Falkirk. Three hundred pounds.

Six   The Incorporation of Shoemakers of Edinburgh. One hundred pounds.

Seven   Frederick Corser, merchant in Dundee. Five hundred pounds.

Eight   George Cruickshank junior, merchant in Aberdeen. Fifty pounds.

Nine   James Dunbar, Baillie of Inverness. One hundred and eighty pounds.

Ten   George Stirling, Doctor of Medicine. Two hundred pounds. (*Signs.*)

Eleven   Sir Archibald Stevenson, Doctor of Medicine. Six hundred pounds. (*Signs. Nods contemptuously at Seventh Subscriber.*)

Twelve   Mr James Gregory, Professor of the Mathematicks in the College of Edinburgh. Eight hundred pounds.

Thirteen   In the name of the Good Town of Edinburgh, the Lord Provost of Edinburgh. Three thousand pounds. (*Signs.*)

Fourteen (*competitively*)   Lord Provost John Anderson, in the name of the City of Glasgow. Three thousand pounds. (*Signs.*)

Song No. 7   Let Scotland's Name (Reprise)

Subscribers   *Let Scotland's name*
Across the world resound
To foreign lands
Where riches abound
One pound today
Tomorrow will be ten
And Scotland will
Be mighty once again.

First Nameless As Subscriber   Was Scotland ever mighty?

Second Nameless As Subscriber   I don't think so.

First Nameless As Subscriber   No, I thought not.

The **Subscribers** *leave.* **Balfour**, **Blackwood** *and* **Borland** *enter, joining* **Paterson** *and* **Mackenzie**. *All others leave. The mood is one of awe rather than triumphalism.*

Paterson   How much, Mr Mackenzie?

Mackenzie   Four hundred thousand pounds.

Blackwood   Four hundred thousand pounds?

Mackenzie   Yes. Four hundred thousand pounds.

Blackwood   Four. Hundred. Thousand?

Paterson   Aye.

Balfour   It is more than half the nation's wealth.

Paterson   Aye.

Mackenzie   It is near enough five times the annual revenue of government.

Paterson   Aye.

Borland   The Lord has smiled upon us. There will be prayers of thanksgiving in every kirk across the land.

Balfour   Four hundred thousand. That sits nicely on the tongue, does it not? Four hundred thousand.

Blackwood   It's a hundred thousand more than three hundred thousand.

All stare at him in their can-he-really-be-this-stupid look.

Blackwood   What we'd hoped to get in London. It's a hundred thousand more than that. We've done better.

Balfour   Oh, right. Well, Scotland aye does better, when we put our minds to it.

Blackwood   Four . . . hundred . . . thousand . . .

Paterson   Yes. (*Silence.*) Gentlemen we are now more powerful than the state.

They contemplate this in silence for a moment.

Paterson   And now, gentleman, it is time for action. There is much work ahead.

Murmuring agreement, they leave.

Paterson   Oh, Mackenzie. A word with you.

He waits for the others to go.

Paterson   A small practical matter . . . at the moment sterling is not a strong currency . . .

Mackenzie   Indeed it is not . . .

Paterson   This weakness of sterling is but a temporary phenomenon, though? Would you not say?

Mackenzie   It can scarcely fall much further.

Paterson   Precisely my view. So. We shall transfer a portion of the Company's assets into Sterling. And when Sterling recovers, we shall transfer it back and make a profit for the company.

Mackenzie   Is that wise, Mr Paterson? No one can absolutely guarantee that the English pound will recover. It might just keep going down and down. There are no guarantees when it comes to currency fluctuations, Mr Paterson.

Paterson   A man can be too careful, you know.

Mackenzie   But to raise all this money, Mr Paterson, with such success, and then to gamble with it. Is that not . . . a step too far?

Paterson   No, no. Now listen, have you ever met James Smyth?

Mackenzie   The London merchant?

Paterson   Yes. A very reliable man.

Mackenzie   A very young man.

Paterson   Young and reliable. And with a shrewd sense of business. I shall charge him with conveying the money to London.

Mackenzie   Have the other directors of the company been consulted?

Paterson   What? Oh, they will have no objection. And we'll limit it to say . . . what shall we say? Twenty-five thousand pounds?

Mackenzie   That is a substantial proportion of our reserves.

Paterson   Yes, and in a few months, when Sterling recovers, then our reserves will be greater than ever before.

Mackenzie   If you say so, Mr Paterson.

Paterson   I do, I do!

From off comes the growing sound of drunken singing. **Paterson** *turns in the direction of the singing.* **Mackenzie** *shakes his head and leaves the other way.*

Scene Thirteen – a street in Edinburgh

Song No. 8   Come Rouse Up Your Hearts

Drunks (*off*)   *Come rouse up your hearts*
　　　　　　　　Come rouse up anon
　　　　　　　　And think of the wisdom of old Solomon
　　　　　　　　And heartily join with our own Paterson
　　　　　　　　To bring home shiploads of treasure.

Four Drunks, *all of them obviously poor, weave slowly and drunkenly across the stage.*

Drunks   *Come rouse up your hearts*
　　　　　　Come rouse up anon
　　　　　　And think of the wisdom of old Solomon
　　　　　　And heartily join with our own Paterson
　　　　　　To bring home shiploads of treasure.

Paterson *looks in the direction of the departing drunks.* **Mrs Paterson** *enters.*

Mrs Paterson   You're a national hero, Mr Paterson.

Paterson   So it would seem.

Mrs Paterson   Does it make you feel proud?

Paterson   In a way.

Mrs Paterson   Does it make you feel afraid?

Paterson   A little.

Mrs Paterson   You've set the whole country aflame.

Paterson   I think I have. (*Turns to look at her.*) You do believe in this venture, don't you?

Mrs Paterson   I believe in you.

Paterson   I hear some . . . reservation.

Mrs Paterson   It will be dangerous.

Paterson   Of course.

Mrs Paterson   You'll make enemies.

Paterson   Courage will be needed. It will be hard. But it can be done. It can be done. It is the pursuit of paradise on earth. All men need to believe in paradise. Some believe it's for the life hereafter. I believe it can also be here on earth. (*Pause.*) You know I will be going with the expedition, don't you?

Mrs Paterson   You've never been one to let other people take all the risks.

Paterson   I will be gone for some long time.

Mrs Paterson   Yes . . . . . as will I.

Paterson (*taken aback*)   Where are you going?

Mrs Paterson   The same place as you.

She takes him by the arm and they walk.

Mrs Paterson   And in our cabin there will be a reposing bed.

Blackout.

Paterson *and* **Mrs Paterson** *leave.*

Scene Fourteen – a workshop in Edinburgh

Underscoring as the stage erupts into purposeful and optimistic busyness. Upstage of the main action we see images of big sailing ships being constructed.

Mackenzie *enters with a shoal of* **Clerks** *following him. Papers are exchanged, signed etc., with* **Mackenzie** *frequently intervening to check something or to sign something off. Huge ledgers are carried about, opened up, filled in, closed, carried off.*

Mackenzie   A contract has been drawn up with Thomas Brown of Edinburgh for one hundred iron spades.

First Clerk   At one shilling and nine pence each.

Mackenzie   One hundred large stocklocks.

First Clerk   At eight pence each.

Mackenzie   One hundred lesser stocklocks.

First Clerk   At four pence each.

Mackenzie   Two hundred chamber doorlocks.

First Clerk   At ten pence each.

Mackenzie   One hundred felling axes.

First Clerk   At one shilling each.

Paterson *enters, sweeps across the stage, followed by* **Balfour** *carrying rolls of plans and piles of documents.*

Paterson   The Endeavour?

Balfour   One hundred and thirty tons. Ten guns.

Paterson   Cost?

Balfour   One thousand eight hundred pounds.

Paterson   Build it.

Balfour   Yes, Mr Paterson!

They leave.

Third Clerk   Mr Robert Arlington to obtain four hundred fishing lines of one hundred fathom in each line.

Second Clerk   William Gray to purchase sufficient amounts of smiths' hammers, anvils, forehammers and bellows.

First Clerk   A letter to be written to Glasgow for patterns of the following particulars: Wooden bowls.

Mackenzie   With their lowest prices.

First Clerk   Horn spoons.

Mackenzie   With their lowest prices.

First Clerk   Smoothing irons.

Mackenzie   With their lowest prices.

First Clerk   White-iron candlesticks.

Mackenzie   With their lowest prices.

Paterson, **Balfour** *and* **Blackwood** *cross the stage.*

Paterson   The Dolphin?

Blackwood   Two hundred tons. Twenty guns . . . No, no, wait, eighteen guns. Sorry.

Paterson   Cost?

Balfour   Two thousand and fifty pounds.

Paterson   Build it.

They leave.

James Smyth *enters, sharply dressed. He is followed by his* **Servant**. *He crosses to* **Mackenzie** *who is engrossed in bookkeeping.*

Smyth   Ah, Mackenzie, here you are. Had the devil of a job finding you. You are Mackenzie, are you not?

Mackenzie   Mr Mackenzie, aye. We have met.

Smyth   Yes. And what an honour it was. And is. And is.

Mackenzie   You will have come about the money that is to be transferred into sterling?

Smyth   How right you are.

Mackenzie   Wait here.

Mackenzie *produces several large keys, goes over to a black cast iron chest and laboriously opens it, making sure that* **Smyth**'*s* *prying eyes cannot see inside. He takes out leather pouches of banknotes, closes and carefully locks the chest.*

Mackenzie   You have an armed escort for the journey to London?

Smyth   Armed to the teeth. No footpad shall have the Company's money, that you can be sure of.

Mackenzie   I'm delighted to hear it. Your instructions are to deposit the money in a sterling account at the Bank of England within twenty-four hours of your arriving in London. If you'll but sign here. And here. And here. And here. And here. And there.

Smyth (*sarcastically*)   Can't be too careful, eh?

Mackenzie   No, you can't.

Smyth (*signs, takes the money*)   Done.

Mackenzie   God speed, Mr Smyth. Goodbye, sir.

Smyth   Goodbye.

Smyth *tosses the leather bags to his* **Servant** *and swaggers off. The* **Servant** *follows, watched balefully by* **Mackenzie**.

First Clerk   Virginia tobacco pipes, two thousand.

Second Clerk   Plaiding hose, four hundred pair.

First Clerk   Fish hooks general purpose, five thousand.

Third Clerk   Cod hooks, three thousand.

Second Clerk   Haddock hooks, three thousand.

Third Clerk   Two hundred and fifty bob wigs.

First Clerk   Six hundred periwigs.

Second Clerk   Thirty dozen pairs of fine loom stockings.

Third Clerk   Forty dozen pairs of kid gloves.

First Clerk   Sixty dozen pairs of woollen gloves.

Second Clerk   One thousand three hundred and eighty Bibles.

Mackenzie   With their lowest prices.

They all write carefully in ledgers.

Song No. 9   Make A List

The Nameless   *When there's nothing must be missed*
                    Make a list
                    Make a list
                    Get the world around you under your control.
                    To make sure that you exist
                    Make a list
                    Make a list
                    A list will help to satisfy your soul
                    Your hungry Presbyterian soul.

                    It's the poetry of profit
                    That will earn you your reward,
                    Diligence and detail will
                    Endear you to the Lord
                    When the Day of Judgment beckons
                    The punishment is swift
                    And your best hope of salvation
                    Is frugality and thrift.

                    It's the poetry of order
                    The romance of neat accounts
                    The road to heaven's measured out
                    In very small amounts.
                    If your ledger's neat and tidy
                    You may conquer all your fears
                    While the jingling of your coin
                    Becomes the music of the spheres.

Paterson, Balfour *and* **Blackwood** *enter.*

Paterson   The Unicorn?

Balfour   Three hundred and twenty tons. Forty guns.

Paterson   Cost?

Blackwood   Eight thousand six hundred pounds.

Paterson   Let it be built.

They leave.

Mackenzie   Sixty horsemen's swords at seven shillings per piece and forty mounted guns at twenty-shillings per piece.

First Clerk   Ordered.

Mackenzie   Dr Munro to proceed to Aberdeen to inform this committee as to the cheapest prices of barrelled codfish.

Second Clerk   He has been told.

The scene gets busier and busier. Maybe instead of remaining on stage the **Clerks** *run in and out.*

First Clerk   John Drummond at his discretion to buy two hundred cows for the Company's use.

Second Clerk   Robert Watson to provide fifteen tons of the best cured pork he can find.

Third Clerk   Daniel Lodge to provide three hundred oxen the best he can find to be slaughtered at Leith.

Paterson, **Balfour** *and* **Blackwood** *enter.*

Paterson   The St Andrew will cost?

Balfour   Eleven thousand five hundred pounds. It is three hundred and fifty tons and will carry forty-eight guns.

Paterson   Good. And the Caledonia?

Balfour   She will cost fifteen thousand pounds.

Blackwood   Six hundred tons and fifty six guns.

Paterson   Let them be built!

They leave.

Second Clerk   Thomas Campbell to provide sixty tuns of good quality cured beef, seven and a half tuns of suet, ten tuns of cheese and ten tuns of butter.

First Clerk   George Clark to provide twelve tuns of Spanish salt, ten barrels of mustard seed, twenty barrels of the best vinegar.

Second Clerk   And forty barrels of brandy.

Third Clerk   And fifty barrels of claret.

First Clerk   Strong claret!

Third Clerk   Strong claret.

The Nameless   *When there's nothing must be missed*
Make a list
Make a list
Get the world around you under your control.
To make sure that you exist
Make a list
Make a list
A list will help to satisfy your soul
Your hungry Presbyterian soul.

It's the poetry of order
The romance of neat accounts
Marking out the course of life
In very small amounts.
If you keep the wages modest
You may conquer half the world
And the neatly folded flag
Will be triumphantly unfurled . . .

Blackout.

Scene Fifteen – the new offices of the Company of Scotland

Paterson *enters with* **Mackenzie** *in tow.*

Paterson   How long will it take to load supplies on to the ships?

Mackenzie   Mr Paterson. There is a matter which –

Paterson   How long?

Mackenzie   I have estimated three weeks, but –

Paterson   Three weeks is too long.

Mackenzie   I have this morning received information concerning –

Paterson   Can it be done in two weeks?

Mackenzie   I am not sure. But there is another matter –

Paterson   I will personally check the condition of the food supplies before the fleet sails.

Mackenzie   Mr Paterson, you may not be allowed to do that!

Paterson   Not allowed? Not allowed? Mackenzie, what are you talking about? I want to check supplies once they are loaded. I don't want to find it's all been so badly stored that half of it's rotten before we even get there. And furthermore –

Mackenzie (*explodes*)   Mr Paterson! The money you sent to London has gone!

Paterson   What?

Mackenzie   The money you sent with Mr Smyth. To be held in sterling. It was never invested. Mr Smyth is thought to be somewhere on the Continent. With twenty-five thousand pounds of the Company's money. Which we are unlikely ever to see again.

Paterson (*dazed*)   He did not convert it into Sterling?

Mackenzie (*shouts*)   Mr Paterson. It has been embezzled. Stolen. Gone.

Paterson   Am I to understand that – ?

Mackenzie   Your reliable Mr Smyth is a common thief.

Paterson   Do the directors know?

Mackenzie   Yes, they know.

Paterson   I will speak with them. (*Leaves followed by* **Mackenzie**.)

Mackenzie (*leaving*)   And they will speak with you.

Scene Sixteen – a coffee house in Edinburgh

We discover the **Directors** *including* **Borland, Erskine, Blackwood** *and* **Balfour** *in the midst of a planning meeting.*

Erskine (*with document*)   So, we are agreed? These seven men will constitute the council which will rule the Colony?

Directors   Agreed.

Erskine   Each Councillor to be given shares in the company to the sum of one thousand two hundred pounds sterling. Agreed?

Directors   Yes, agreed.

Erskine   Each colonist will be given fifty acres of fertile land for cultivation. Gentlemen to be given a hundred acres. Councillors to be given a hundred and fifty acres. Agreed?

Directors   Aye. Yes.

Paterson (*entering*)   Gentlemen, what is this about the stores? It has always been clear that the loading of the stores will be supervised by me. I propose –

Borland   We may not wish to know what you propose, Mr Paterson.

Blackwood   I find this very difficult to admit, Mr Paterson, but our faith in you . . . is . . . well, it is . . . damaged.

Balfour   And you know how much I admire you, but to entrust such a sum . . .

Borland   Without consulting us.

Blackwood   Without consulting us.

Erskine   We will keep this information from the public.
A new call on funds will have to be made. We shall say it is
because of the great success of the previous call.

Paterson   I wish to discuss the provisions. And how they
are stored. As a councillor, I have the right to –

Balfour   You are not a Councillor.

Paterson (*incredulous*)   I am not a Councillor?

Balfour   I am sorry. We cannot have the colony ruled by
men who are careless with the Company's money.

Paterson   Careless? I was not careless, Mr Balfour. I was
working to enrich the Company.

Borland   By taking risks. No fear of risk. That is your
weakness, Mr Paterson.

Paterson   Do not lecture me, Mr Borland. Your abilities are
too modest to permit you to lecture William Paterson. And
who is to be councillor in my stead?

Erskine   I am.

Paterson   You? You? (*To others.*) You have chosen Erskine as
a Councillor?

Balfour   Aye, we have.

Paterson (*to* **Erskine**)   You who've shown so little belief in
this undertaking?

Erskine   I have an investment to protect. From incompetent
men.

Balfour   We all have investments to protect.

Blackwood   Aye. That's why we have put Mr Erskine in
charge of the supplies. Your proposed inspection will not be
necessary.

Paterson *grabs the list, looks at the names.*

Paterson   These are our councillors? These are their names?

Erskine   Yes.

Paterson *laughs.*

Paterson (*in mocking disbelief*)   Major James Cunningham? He is to be a Councillor of the Colony?

Blackwood   He's a most reliable and upright gentleman.

Paterson   James Cunningham has never been out of Scotland!

Balfour   He is a true patriot.

Paterson   He knows nothing about ships. He knows nothing about trade. And his military experience is restricted to taking part in the massacre of Glencoe.

Borland   The man is a pillar of the kirk.

Paterson   Oh, and is that intended to be a recommendation?

Borland   Do not speak thus, Mr Paterson!

Paterson (*reads*)   John Montgomerie?! Good God. Are you mad?

Balfour   His uncle is Lord of the Treasury.

Blackwood   I like his uncle a great deal, actually. Very nice man. Has a most beautiful house near Inverness. With very fine hedges.

Paterson   Robert Jolly . . .

Balfour   Ship's captain.

Paterson   Retired ship's captain! He hasn't commanded a ship for twelve years. William Vetch. No qualifications whatsoever.

Borland   His father and I studied divinity together.

Paterson (*stares at document*)   You have made Robert Pennicuick Commodore of the Fleet?!

Erskine   I know him well.

Paterson   Oh. Then you will know he is a lover of strong drink. That he is hated by the men under his command. How many servants did he insist on taking? . . . Come on, tell me! . . .

Balfour   None at all.

Blackwood (*blurts it out*)   Five. (*Realises.*) Sorry.

Paterson   Only five. You are fortunate.

Erskine   Stop this, Mr Paterson.

Paterson   You fools.

Balfour   The Board of Directors appointed the best possible people.

Paterson   The Board of Directors appointed its friends. Behind my back. These are decisions you will long regret.

Erskine   We remain grateful to you, Mr Paterson. It's your vision that has made this noble undertaking possible. Of course we realise that you will no longer wish to sail with the expedition. But your counsels will be greatly valued here in Edinburgh and when the fleet returns –

Paterson   I do not think you know me well enough, Mr Erskine. When the fleet sails, I will be aboard it.

He leaves. The **Directors** *leave from the opposite side.*

Scene Seventeen – a piece of land overlooking the port of Leith.

Off. Crowd noises.

Song No. 10   Let Scotland's Name (Reprise)

Singers (*off*)   *Let Scotland's name*
Across the world resound
To foreign lands
Where riches abound

One pound today
Tomorrow will be ten
And Scotland will
Be mighty once again.

The melody continues as underscoring, or maybe continues to be
sung as if coming from far away. **Paterson** *and* **Mrs Paterson**
enter, ready for the journey, **Servants** *carrying luggage.*

Mrs Paterson   Listen. You hear them?

Paterson   Yes.

Mrs Paterson   They are gathering in their thousands to
watch the fleet set sail. Everywhere. On Castle Hill. On
Caltoun Crags. Never has Leith seen so many people.

Mackenzie (*entering*)   Mr Paterson. Mrs Paterson. You must
hurry. It will take time to get through the crowds. There's
more want to go than there are places. They're finding
dozens of men hidden in the ships and removing them by
force. There's men pleading and begging to be allowed to
go, clinging to the ropes and timbers till the very last
moment. Beacons are to be lit all the way up the east coast
to mark the progress of the fleet. The country has known
nothing like it, Mr Paterson. Nothing.

Paterson   We will be there shortly.

Mackenzie   As soon as possible please, Mr Paterson.
(*Leaves.*)

Paterson   My dear?

He holds out his arm. She takes it. They leave followed by the
Servants*. The cheering crowds get louder. Church bells. Then this*
dips as a **Poor Girl** *appears and sings.*

Song No. 11   Auspicious Day

Poor Girl   *On this auspicious day*
                    The valiant Scots display
                    Their colours to the world.

Chorus	*The door of the seas* *The keys of the universe.*
Poor Girl	*May Neptune favour them* *With wind and tide* *And may the Lord provide* *Protection from the storm.*
Chorus	*The door of the seas* *The keys of the universe.*
Poor Girl	*The St Andrew* *The Endeavour* *And the Dolphin all set sail* *Caledonia sets sail* *And the Unicorn sets sail.* *All ships and men* *Directed by the hand of God.*
Chorus	*The door of the seas* *The keys of the universe* *The door of the seas* *The keys of the universe* *Will be ours* *Will be Scotland's* *Will be ours.*
Poor Girl	*And so our country's darkest night is gone* *And Scotland stands* *To greet a glorious dawn.*

As the music soars to match the vision of the closing words, a
Spanish Soldier *enters downstage left. He watches silently for a*
few seconds, then turns and leaves.

Chorus / Poor Girl	*Our country's darkest night is gone* *And Scotland stands* *To greet a glorious dawn.*

Blackout.

Interval.

Act Two

Scene One – on board the Caledonia

Members of the **Crew** *turn the capstain or pull on ropes.*
One **Sailor** *takes the solo part, while everyone else joins in the*
chorus.

Song No. 12   Sea Shanty

Sailor   *A sailor lad from Aberdeen*
            Was handsome tall and strong

Crew   *Hey, hey, hey, high, ho.*

Sailor   *He met a whore from Amsterdam*
            And swived her all night long

Crew   *Now there's fire down below*

Sailor   *He swived that whore from Amsterdam*
            And never got a kiss

Crew   *Hey, hey, hey, high, ho.*

Sailor   *But ever since he swived her*
            He's afraid to take a piss

Crew   *'Cause there's fire down below.*
            Fire down below me lads,
            Fire down below.

Sailor   *A gentleman from London*
            Was so scraggy and so thin

Crew   *Hey, hey, hey, high, ho*

Sailor   *She didn't even notice*
            When he tried to slip it in

The **Rev. Borland** *appears upstage of them, Bible in clasped*
hands, and in blissful ignorance smilingly observes. They don't
notice his presence. He sways to the music.

Crew   *But there's fire down below.*
Fire down below, me lads,
Fire down below.

Sailor   A *farming man from Inverness*
Preferred his whoories cheap

Crew   *Hey, hey, hey, high, ho.*

Sailor   *If they asked for too much money*
He'd go off and find a sheep.

Borland *frowns, a bit worried, but doesn't quite get it.*

Crew   *And there's fire down below.*

Sailor   *A Church of Scotland Minister*
Was riding with the hunt

Crew   *Hey, hey, hey, high, ho.*

Borland *gets it.*

Sailor   *He wasn't hunting deer*
What he was hoping for . . . was . . .

The **Sailor** *has caught sight of* **Borland** *and stops singing.*
Borland *gazes fiercely at him for a few seconds. The* **Crew** *realise*
what's going on and jump into the chorus.

Crew   *And there's fire down below.*

Borland *stands staring a moment longer and then turns in disgust*
and walks off. The **Crew** *pause till he has gone, then they all tip-toe*
off, singing in a loud whisper.

Sailor   *A Church of Scotland Minister*
Was riding with the hunt

Crew   *Hey, hey, hey, high, ho.*

Sailor   *He wasn't hunting deer*
What he was hoping for was . . . (mouths) *cunt.*

They leave.

Music.

The ship is now under full sail. **Paterson** *appears, followed by* **Erskine***.*

Paterson   No, Mr Erskine, I do not get seasick.

Erskine   But I do, Mr Paterson, I do.

Paterson   Ah, well. Worry not. (*Cheerfully.*) In my experience the first six weeks are the worst.

Erskine *runs to the side of the ship, leans over and retches.*

Paterson   That is a terrible waste of food, Mr Erskine, a terrible waste. We're short enough of rations as it is.

Erskine (*weakly*)   You're not a man of great sympathies, are you?

Paterson   The voyage does not appear to incommode my wife. If a mere woman can cope, I'm sure you can too.

Erskine   Your wife is no mere woman.

Paterson   In any case, a little seasickness is nothing. It's the flux and the fever you need to be afraid of.

Erskine *runs to the side again, retches.*

Paterson   Dear, oh dear.

Mackenzie *appears.*

Paterson   Mackenzie. How fares our Captain this fine morning?

Mackenzie   I wish we had sailed upon the Endeavour. There is much to be said for a ship's captain who is sober for at least a few hours a day.

Paterson   I agree. But not being a Councillor . . . well, I'm in no position to choose which ship we sail in.

Mackenzie   It's a shame and a scandal how you have been treated, Mr Paterson. Without you, this whole venture –

Paterson   Yes, yes. (*Sees* **Erskine** *approaching.*) Voided to your heart's content, Mr Erskine?

Erskine   Mr Paterson, since we have little choice but to spend many weeks together in cramped and difficult circumstances, might it be wiser if you chose not to mock those afflicted by seasickness?

Paterson   Oh, Mr Erskine, you would deprive me of what small pleasures are left to me?

Erskine   Now listen, sir, and listen well. I believe in this expedition.

Paterson   Oh? Why then did you not take the trouble to ensure that the food was stored properly? Only three weeks into our voyage and the men already on reduced rations? A quarter of our stores are rotted. It was foolishness. And it need not have happened. I told you how the supplies needed to be stowed, Mr Erskine, I told you! I have experience of such things. And did you listen? Did you?

Erskine   No, I did not. It was my fault. I am sorry.

Paterson (*surprised*)   Oh . . . well, it is a strong man who admits to his errors. But I am puzzled, Mr Erskine. It doesn't seem to me that your heart has ever fully been engaged in this endeavour.

Erskine   It was not, to begin with. You persuaded me. I was not convinced. And you persuaded me. After the matter of James Smyth and the missing funds, well, I could no longer see you as Councillor. But that is the sort of man you are, Paterson. You have ideas. You have vision. You have courage. And then you go too far. Always one step too far, Mr Paterson. That is why I am on board. To protect you from yourself.

Paterson (*bows slightly*)   How kind of you.

Erskine   Let us work together, sir. For the sake of Darien. For the sake of Scotland.

He holds out his hand. **Paterson** *stares at it for a moment, then takes it.* **Pennicuick** *appears.* **Erskine** *leaves.*

Pennicuick   Paterson! Good morning!

Paterson   Captain Pennicuick. What a pleasure. We are making good progress?

Pennicuick   Well enough, sir. By my reckoning we are some twenty leagues ahead of the rest of the fleet.

Paterson   It is a tribute to your navigational skills, Captain.

Mackenzie *stifles a laugh.* **Pennicuick** *shoots him a sharp glance.*

Pennicuick   What mean you by that?

Paterson   I mean that you have difficulty reading the navigation tables.

Pennicuick   Arrant nonsense, sir.

Paterson   I have watched you. All I can say is that I am grateful for the first mate. He seems to be competent in the use of the astrolabe. So they'll never make *him* a captain, eh?

Pennicuick   It's time for my breakfast. (*Makes to leave.*)

Paterson (*quietly*)   Is that what you call it?

Borland *enters.*

Borland   Captain Pennicuick. Do not go.

Pennicuick   But I have need of my breakfast.

Borland   We all know what your breakfast consists of Captain. Half a bottle of rum.

Pennicuick   That is not true, sir. That is absolutely not true. It is normally half a bottle of brandy. (*Laughs at his own joke.*)

Borland   Your men are out of control. They sing lewd and profane songs.

Pennicuck   They are sailors, Reverend. Their lives are hard. Harder than yours has ever been. Or ever will be. They are at sea for months at a time. Of course their songs are lewd. So would yours be if you hadn't swived a woman in three months . . . Aye, well in your case, maybe the argument doesn't quite hold up. Now if you'll excuse me . . . breakfast. (*Leaves.*)

Borland   Mr Paterson. The men seem to respect you . . .

Mackenzie   They do, Mr Borland, they do.

Borland   So if our Captain will not admonish them, you must do so, Mr Paterson. These men must be chastised for their dissolute behaviour. The Lowlanders are bad enough. But the Highlanders are yet worse. They keep themselves to themselves, drinking their abominable usquebaugh and no doubt secretly muttering their hocus pocus and pledging loyalty to the Pope in Rome.

Paterson   There is something you must know, Mr Borland. I am not greatly concerned about a man's religion.

Borland   Not greatly concerned?!

Paterson   Like you, sir, I am glad we have thrown off the chains of Rome. Many died to make that possible. But I observe that those who are ardent in pursuing their own religious freedom are often equally ardent in denying it to others.

Mackenzie   Mr Paterson, take care.

Borland   Do not speak of freedom, sir. Man is too base to be permitted the burden of freedom. Such is the furious rage of man's corrupt nature that unless severe punishment be appointed and malefactors controlled, it were better that man live among brutes and wild beasts than among men.

Paterson   I have higher hopes for mankind, Mr Borland. You should know, sir, that Darien will not merely be a little Scotland. It will a better place.

Borland   Better than Scotland?

Paterson   Aye, a better world. Where men may worship as they please, without fear of persecution.

Borland (*intimate*)   You are not . . . you are not a
freethinker, are you, sir?

Paterson   I care not what I am called. I only know that no
man should be tortured and persecuted for the sake of his
faith.

Borland   I will hear no more of this. (*Leaves.*)

The **Nameless** *as* **Sailors** *enter with buckets and long-handled
scrubbing brushes or mops. They pour out liquid and begin to wash
and scrub the decks.*

First Nameless   I never really wanted to play the part of a
sailor.

Second Nameless   Oh, I suppose you wanted to be King
William, did you?

First Nameless   Aye, King William, that'd have done me
fine.

Third Nameless   You could never be a King William. Look
at you.

Second Nameless (*looks at* **First Nameless**)   He's right you
know.

Fourth Nameless   I'd like to play a rich man in Edinburgh.
You know, one of them who spends all day in coffee houses
telling people why it's only right and proper he earns about
two thousand times what I do.

First Nameless   That'd be nice.

Second Nameless   Aye, that'd be nice.

They continue swabbing the decks. **Mrs Paterson** *enters.*

Mrs Paterson   Oh, that smell of vinegar again. It's worse
than the smell below decks. Well, almost.

Paterson   It keeps the fever at bay.

Mrs Paterson   Does it? Since leaving Leith fourteen men
have died. And one of the Councillors gravely ill.

Paterson   Fourteen is fewer than you'd expect for a voyage of this duration. But I would still have them wash down the decks with vinegar every day. Unfortunately the men know they can get away with twice a week. They have no respect for our captain. And why should they?

Mrs Paterson   Will, have you considered . . . ? If this Councillor should die . . . ?

Paterson   How mean you?

Mrs Paterson   If he should die, they are obliged to elect a replacement.

Paterson   They will want me? Is that what you mean to say?

Mrs Paterson   It is. You have been proven right on so many things. In their hearts they know it. They know that their safety depends on men like you. Men whose vision is not clouded by stupidity. Or by drink. Men who are where they are because of merit, not because of rank or connections. I hope you will write in your journal how they have treated you.

Paterson   My journal should not be a litany of complaint.

Mrs Paterson   But history must know the truth.

The **Sailors** *stop swabbing the deck.*
Lighting change.
Music.
The ship is becalmed.
Paterson *sits writing in his journal. The* **Sailors** *come downstage and become the* **Nameless**.

Song No. 13   The Nameless of the Earth (Partial Reprise)

First Nameless   *All history is written*
By those who can write
Can read and can write
So history
Is normally
Black and white.

Mrs Paterson	*And then*
	It's written by men
All Nameless & Mrs Paterson	*And so we fear*
	That we may disappear
	Unknown
	Unsung
	The nameless of the earth
	Despised
	Forgotten
	Of little worth
	Yet hoping that our voices can
	be heard.
	Hoping that every now and then
	The nameless of the earth can
	still be heard
	Can dream at least
	Of one day being invited to the
	feast.

*During the last few lines of the number, the **Sailors** carry on a dead body sewn into a sailcloth. Behind comes **Pennicuick** with prayer book and then the **Rev Borland**, open Bible in his hands. The body is committed to the deep.*

Borland   Most merciful father we beseech thee of thine infinite goodness to give us grace to live in thy fear and love and to die in thy favour, that when the judgement shall come we may be found acceptable in thy sight through the love of thy Son, our Saviour, Jesus Christ. Amen.

*The **Sailors** disperse.*

Pennicuick   Tis the second one, today, Mr Borland. Could we not maybe combine them, so as to . . . you know . . . save time . . . ?

Borland   We have just buried a Councillor of the Colony, Captain. I will thank you to show a little respect.

Pennicuick   Aye, you're right.

Borland   Although, of course, every man is equal in the sight of God.

Pennicuick (*unconvinced*)   Aye. (*Pause.*) Would you care for a wee brandy? No, no, I suppose you wouldn't.

Borland   Your constant tippling is an abomination, Captain.

Pennicuick   An abomination?

Borland   Yes.

Pennicuick   Is it that bad?

Borland   Yes, it is.

Pennicuick   Aye, well, I'd better get back to my cabin. For a wee abomination. (*Leaves.*)

Music.

Borland *remains on deck.* **Erskine** *enters.* **First Councillor** *enters.* **Mackenzie** *enters, carrying a foolscap leather-bound book.*

Mackenzie   Gentlemen, following the death of one of your fellow Councillors, you are obliged under Chapter Seven of the constitution of the Company of Scotland, to agree upon a replacement forthwith.

There is an awkward silence.

Borland   I suppose we're mean to appoint Paterson, are we?

Mackenzie   The choice is yours gentlemen, not mine. Perhaps you'd prefer Captain Pennicuick?

Borland   That is an ill-judged jest, Mackenzie.

Erskine   Aye, but it reveals a truth, does it not? As everybody is aware, I have had my difficulties with Mr Paterson. But he has experience. And knowledge. And has been the moving spirit of this enterprise.

Borland   I have no doubt as to the competence of the man. But will he uphold the word of God?

Erskine   That is your job, Mr Borland. I propose that we appoint Paterson.

First Councillor   I agree.

Erskine   We will better be able to control the man.

Borland   Maybe . . .

Mackenzie   So it is agreed?

Erskine   Yes.

First Councillor   Yes.

Borland   Aye . . . well . . . all right.

Mackenzie   Mr Paterson is appointed Councillor of the Colony of Darien.

All leave except **Mackenzie**. **Paterson** *enters and he and* **Mackenzie** *shake hands warmly. They leave.*
Time passes.
Music.

The **Sailors** *appear. There follows a movement sequence, slow and languid, a sense of time hanging heavy in the hot air as the ship moves slowly.* **Paterson** *enters, watches the sailors in silence for a moment.*

Paterson   Men. Can I say a few words to you?

They groan and show reluctance to listen.

Paterson   It's nigh on four months since we left home. It's been hard. It is hard. You've all left behind family, and friends, sweethearts.

Second Sailor (*points to another sailor*)   *He* hasn't! (*Laughter.*)

Paterson   Every voyage is hard. I know that. I've sailed half around the globe in my time. Seen storms and shipwrecks. Looked starvation in the face. Smelt the stench of death below decks. Watched men die. Watched many men die. So it is on every voyage. And yet . . . this voyage is different. Aye, it's full of dangers, I never said otherwise. But think what awaits us. A new land. A new life. A life of plenty. An escape from want. An escape from famine. To a new land waiting to be tamed. By us. We will find ourselves in one of the most healthful, rich and fruitful countries upon earth, situated between two vast oceans, which means Darien can become the emporium for the treasures of half the world. Men, you will be rich. You will be the rich and famous sons of Scotland. In centuries to come, you will be remembered as the men who created a new Scotland. A Scotland of wealth and power and confidence. All founded upon the land of Darien, where glory awaits you. Glory – and gold. So be brave as I know you are. Bold and brave. My men. And with you I will share not only the gold, I will share with you the dangers. This is my word.

Song No. 14   Time To Be Bold

First Sailor   *Time to be bold, me lads,*
Time to be bold,
Time to think of better times to come.
Think about the gold, me lads,
Think about the gold,
Think about the women and the rum.

Second Sailor   *Maybe we'll find fortune*

Third Sailor   *Maybe we'll find fame*

Fourth Sailor   *Maybe we'll find nothing*
And wish that we were hame

Fifth Sailor   *Maybe we'll meet Spaniards*
And we'll find out how they feel
About taking in their bellies
A length of Scottish steel

Sixth Sailor   *Maybe we'll meet natives*
In a land that time forgot

First Sailor   *But maybe they'll have women*
Who'll be hungry for a Scot

All Sailors   *Aye we're sure that there are better times to come.*

First Sailor   *So think about the gold, me lads.*

All Sailors   *Think about the gold.*
And could we have another round of rum?

Lookout   Land ahoy!

Music.

Scene Two – Darien

Lighting change as we go into an impressionistic rendering of a romantic paradise. On the sound track we hear rowing boats, shouted commands, surf. Then exotic tropical rainforest sounds – insects, birds, frogs, toads, other animals.

Borland *leads the hymn-singing.*

Song No. 15   What Should We Do But Sing His Praise

Borland & Others   *What should we do but sing His praise*
Who led us through the watery maze
And brought us safe ashore?
To God above we give our thanks
And praise him evermore.

Paterson   And now, by virtue of the powers granted unto us, we do here settle, and in the name of God establish ourselves. And we do name the city which we here shall build New Edinburgh.

Cheering.

Paterson   And we do name the fort which we shall here build Fort St Andrew.

Cheering.

Paterson   And for the honour and the memory of the most ancient and renowned name of our Mother Kingdom, we

do and will from henceforth call this country of Darien by
the name of Caledonia.

Cheering.

Paterson   And ourselves and our successors, by the name
of Caledonians!

Prolonged cheering. **Borland** *tries to impose his will. But the
atmosphere is raucous.*

Borland   Well will now sing . . . we will now sing . . . We
will now sing Hymn number . . .

A **Colonist** *launches into a song.*

Song No. 16   Come Rouse Up Your Hearts (Reprise)

Colonist   *Come rouse up your hearts*
Come rouse up anon . . .

Others *join in.* **Borland** *is forced to give up.*

Colonists   *And think of the wisdom of old Solomon*
And heartily join with our own Paterson
To bring home shiploads of treasure.
Come rouse up your hearts
Come rouse up anon
And think of the wisdom of old Solomon
And heartily join with our own Paterson
To bring home shiploads of treasure.

*We go into a choreographed scene of multiple discoveries. Awe-struck
and excited* **Colonists** *report and exchange information about what
they have seen.*

Mackenzie   There are cedar trees in great abundance.

Erskine   And also mahogany.

Mackenzie   And lignum vitae and yellow sanders.

First Colonist   Two leagues hence we met about twenty
Indians with bows and lances.

Second Colonist   But when we approached, they unstrung their bows in token of friendship.

First Colonist   One of us gave us this. (*Shows a penis cover.*)

Second Colonist   It is gold!

Erskine   Gold?! Let me see . . . Yes, I believe it is gold!

Mackenzie   Gold!

Second Colonist   What use do they make of such a thing?

First Colonist *holds it over the front of his trousers. There is ribald laughter.*

Mackenzie   Did you have to give them anything in return?

First Colonist   We gave them a hat, a wig and a Bible.

Second Colonist   One of them spoke a few words of Spanish. As far as we could understand, they do not love the Spaniard. They are pleased that we are here.

First Colonist   I saw a river. It may be the river where they pan for gold!

All   Gold!

First Colonist   There are wild hogs!

Second Colonist   That may be eaten! And a kind of partridge. And fish in the rivers. This big!

First Colonist   And a large bird with a pouch under its throat where it can store the fish it catches.

Second Colonist   The natives call it a pec-ilan.

First Colonist   A pel-ican!

Second Colonist   Yes.

The **Rev. Borland** *arrives. They ignore him or do not notice him.*

Erskine   The ground is fertile and rich. They grow cocoa, for the making of chocolate.

Mackenzie   They also grow vanilla. And sugar cane. And maize.

Erskine   And oranges.

Mackenzie   And oranges.

First Colonist   Plantains. Yams.

Third Colonist (*arriving*)   The women wear no clothes! The women wear no clothes!

All   Hooray!

First Colonist   Where are they, where are they?

Second Colonist   Is it far?

First Colonist   Did you bring me one?

Second Colonist   Any nice young virgins to be had? I don't want one that's been swived by a Spaniard.

Third Colonist   Aye, let's hope there's enough virgins to go round.

Borland (*scandalised*)   You filthy immoral degenerate creatures! Sinners! Sinners, all of you! Sinners! Think not that you can escape God's wrath by coming to this place. This is Scottish soil now. Christian soil!

Pennicuick *emerges, a bottle in his hand and blearily observes.*

Borland   And let me tell you, in case you do not know, it is the local custom that if a man debauches another man's wife, they thrust a briar into the passage of his member, and turn it round a dozen times.

Colonists *all wince noisily.*

Borland   Aye, that will make you hesitate, though eternal damnation should make you hesitate yet more.

Pennicuick   Well said, Reverend.

Borland   And you, Captain Pennicuick are a disgrace. A drunken disgrace to the name of Scotland.

Pennicuick   You see that briar you just talked about? Why don't you stick one up your pious Presbyterian arse?

The conflict is defused as **Paterson** *enters purposefully with maps. He is followed by* **Erskine***.* **Paterson** *spreads out the maps. They sit down on barrels / packing cases.* **Borland** *remains a little apart from the others.*

Paterson   There is a natural harbour . . . here. On one side of it there's a peninsula of flat sandy ground, of about thirty acres in extent. There we shall build our capital city.

Pennicuick   Let me see, let me see. Oh aye, excellent, excellent.

Erskine   And to defend it?

Paterson   We must build a fort. But before that we shall erect a battery of fifteen heavy guns. They can both defend the city from the land and also command the harbour entrance.

Pennicuick   Yes, good. Good.

Mrs Paterson *joins them. All except* **Paterson** *look a bit put out.*

Paterson   Now. At its narrowest part this little peninsula here is only two hundred paces wide.

Erskine   We make a cutting through it!

Paterson   Exactly. A deep cutting to let in the sea. Our capital city will thus be on an island, and safe from attack on all sides. Once this has been established, we will survey the isthmus and plan the building of our trading road to link the two oceans.

Mrs Paterson   Huts for the sick. That is the first thing. Land must be cleared and huts built for those who are sick.

Mr Paterson   You are right. Mr Erskine. Will you take command of the building of these huts?

Erskine   I am already in command of building the fort.

Mrs Paterson   Yes, and now you are being asked also to be in command of building the huts.

Erskine   Has Mrs Paterson been appointed Councillor? I was not aware she was empowered to give commands. To men.

Paterson   Think of it as a suggestion, Mr Erskine. And then do it.

Borland (*intervening*)   We will need to keep a firm grip on the morals of the men in this place.

Mrs Paterson   You've always been an ambitious person, Mr Borland.

Mackenzie (*comes running, excited*)   Mr Paterson, Mr Paterson! (*Struggling to get his breath.*) There is a French sloop in the bay. They are sailing to Jamaica tomorrow. They can take our letters. From there they can be put on a ship bound for Bristol. With luck and a fair wind Edinburgh will have news of us in only three months from now!

Paterson   That's excellent, Mackenzie. Well done. Tell everyone they have half a day to write to their loved ones. Let those who are lettered help those who are not. As for us, we have reports to write. Reports that will bring cheer to every man and woman in Scotland.

Scene Three – Darien

Music.
Darkness.
Music.
The sound track is now the rainforest at night – threatening and sinister. Strange howls and screeches. It is dark, and raining heavily. By the light of an oil lamp two **Gravediggers**. *As the darkness very slowly gives way to in the torrential rain (thunder and lightning?) we a short row of simple wooden crosses. The two* **Gravediggers** *leave. Day breaks. The sounds change. Steam rises*

from the jungle. Sheltered under an awning are **Erskine**,
Pennicuick *and* **Paterson**, *squinting at a map. The rain thunders
down. Each entry of the* **Gravediggers** *marks a time jump in the
conversation.*

Paterson It should have been built by now, Mr Erskine.

Erskine The land is difficult to build upon.

Paterson As I told you it would be. You have chosen the
wrong spot.

Pennicuik *pours himself a brandy, thereby discovering the bottle
is empty.*

Erskine Captain Pennicuick and I think it the best spot.

Paterson It's a swamp. A morass. You couldn't even grow
anything there, far less build a fort upon it.

Penniciuik It has easy access for the ships.

Paterson Is that your only concern?

Pennicuick No. I'd like some more brandy. (*Shouts.*) Boy!

The **Gravediggers** *enter carrying a simple wooden cross, which
they hammer into the ground.*

Erskine They need to work faster.

Paterson You want the men to work faster? In this heat?
This humidity? Without proper rations?

Pennicuick We'll unload a few more barrels of salted pork.

Paterson It's uneatable. Not fit for dogs. It's green and
stinking and riddled with maggots.

Pennicuick Give it to the Highlanders. Better than boiled
oats, eh?

Paterson I notice your own fare does not include rotting
pork.

Pennicuik Indeed it does not. If the men want decent
food, they must get on with clearing the land and planting.

Paterson They are weakened by disease. Made ill by this unrelenting rainfall. The land is not so easily cleared as once we thought.

Erskine And whose fault is that? Who made us believe we were coming to an earthly paradise?

Paterson *looks away. The* **Gravediggers** *enter carrying a simple wooden cross, which they hammer into the ground.*

Paterson Why are all the supplies being kept on board the ships?

Erskine So that they remain dry.

Paterson No. The Councillors are sitting in the ships controlling the supply of food. And keeping the best for themselves.

Pennicuik Why, would you want us to keep the worst for ourselves? (*Laughs at his own wit. Waves a glass in the air.*) Boy!

The **Gravediggers** *enter carrying a simple wooden cross, which they hammer into the ground.*

Pennicuick Now just hold on, Mr Paterson. You want us to leave our cabins and sleep in yon half-built huts among the noxious vapours of the mangrove swamps?

Paterson It's what I'm going to do henceforth.

Erskine You are being foolish.

Paterson The men need leadership. They will respond. We have suffered setbacks. They can be overcome. It can be done. It can be done. (*Gets up to go.*)

Pennicuick I will have more brandy. Boy!

The **Boy** *arrives, pours out a very large brandy.*

Pennicuick *leaves, followed by* **Erskine***.* **Paterson***, alone on stage, takes in the wooden crosses, turns comes downstage. Contemplating failure – or perhaps trying to drive the thought away – he stands in the rain until he is soaked.*

Scene Four – the Company Offices, Edinburgh

Off: a horse galloping. **Balfour** *and* **Blackwood** *look up.*
A **Messenger** *enters, big leather knapsack over one shoulder.*
He hands **Blackwood** *and* **Balfour** *packages in heavy oiled paper.*
With trembling hands **Blackwood** *opens a sheaf of letters.*
He reads.

Blackwood   They are safe. They are well.

Balfour   Thanks be to God.

Balfour *tears open other letters. They exchange news of the contents.*

Blackwood   They made landfall in Darien exactly as planned. No ships lost. Only twenty-eight men dead on the voyage over.

Balfour (*reading*)   The land is fertile and fruitful!

Blackwood (*reading*)   The climate is benign!

Balfour (*reading*)   They are building a fort to be known as Fort St Andrew!

Blackwood (*reading*)   And a capital city to be known as New Edinburgh!

Balfour *turns to the* **Horseman**.

Balfour   Convey this news to Parliament. Tell the Lord High Chancellor that Scotland has an empire!

The **Horseman** *bows briefly and leaves.*

Balfour   Oh, what a day, what a day for Scotland. May God bless this country. And God bless you, Mr Blackwood! (*Emotional, he embraces* **Blackwood**, *then feels embarrassed and steps back stiffly.*) Sorry, sorry. Got a wee bit carried away.

Music begins. **Tweedale** *appears in full regalia*

Tweedale   Let us give thanks to Almighty God that the Darien expedition has been crowned with success! Let there be prayers said in every church in the land. A service of thanksgiving in St Giles Cathedral. Let all Scotland rejoice. Let riders be sent to every corner of the land to promulgate the happy news. Let the guns of the Half Moon battery be fired across the North Loch. Let bonfires be lit at Holyrood and at the Netherbow port. And tonight, tonight issue an order that candles are to be displayed in every window in the High Street.

Song No. 17   Oh Caledonia

Singers (*off*)   *Oh Caledonia*
Your glory we proclaim
Soon all mankind
Will recognise thy fame
An end to poverty
An end to shame
Dear Caledonia
We praise thy name.

Lights go down and we see the High Street of Edinburgh with candles in the windows. Church bells ring out. Cheering crowds in the distance.

Scene Five – Darien

Off: for a few moments the previous song may continue. **Paterson** *enters followed by* **Erskine**.

Paterson   How often do I have to tell you? Once we start trading, all will be well. We did not choose Darien for its beauty or its ease. We chose it because it is our key to trading across the isthmus.

Erskine   We did not choose Darien. You chose Darien, Mr Paterson. You told us there would be gold, and what have we found so far? A few bits and pieces of native ornamentation – some of it unmentionable in polite circles. You did not tell us about the mangrove swamps. Or the disease. Or the heat and the humidity.

Paterson   Did you think you were coming to a piece of Scotland, Mr Erskine? Did it not occur to you that the climate might be different? You are part of this now, remember, Mr Erskine. We are in this together.

Erskine   Aye, I know. But men are dying of the fever every day. There is weariness. There is despair. Hope can only take you so far, you know. It is a commodity that is not endless in its supply. Except in your case.

Paterson   We always knew it would be hard at the start. We always knew that men would die.

Erskine   And did you say that to them?

Paterson   They knew! They know. These men have fled famine and starvation. They know the meaning of danger. But this is danger with the possibility of a great and glorious outcome.

Erskine   Glorious . . . (*shakes his head*).

Mackenzie *enters.*

Mackenzie   We have conversed with the Indians. Not without some difficulty I must confess. Some speak a few words of Spanish, but . . . well, my Spanish is not of the best. But they also have a language of gesture. It is most ingenious.

Erskine   Will you come to the point, Mr Mackenzie?

Mackenzie   Do you know how they express the passing of time? It is thus: (*performs a mime of his hand crossing the sky, and ending with his head against the pillow of his hands*). That is a day and a night. Twenty-four hours. And we have established how many days' march it is to cross from here to the Pacific Ocean.

Erskine   How many?

Mackenzie   This many.

Paterson *watches in fascination as* **Mackenzie** *laboriously performs the mime of six days.*

Erskine (*mutters*)   Oh, in heaven's name.

Paterson   Six?

Mackenzie   Six.

Paterson   Only six days' march to traverse the peninsula! Did you hear that Mr Erskine?

Erskine   Aye.

Mackenzie   It is good news. Excellent news.

Paterson   Even Mr Erskine will acknowledge that. Think. If the isthmus can be crossed through the jungle in only six days, imagine . . . once we have cleared a trail . . . goods can be transported swiftly . . . we will look back on our early difficulties and wonder why we ever had a single doubt.

Erskine *stares bleakly at him.*

Scene Six – the Court of King William

William *arranges hair and clothes in mirror, trying on different articles of clothing, helped by* **Joost**.

William   Well, who would have thought it? The Scotchmen have landed, eh? And thriving, I hear?

Joost   So we are informed, your Majesty. There is much rejoicing in Edinburgh.

William   I suppose that means 'much drinking' . . . ? Not that one. The blue one. Do pay attention, Joost. This 'colony' of theirs. It is engaged in trade?

Joost   That is certainly what they intend.

William   Shall I leave the Spaniard to deal with them, shall we, Joost? That would be convenient.

Joost   The Spanish have ships on the coast. And soldiers. But they hesitate to attack. The Scotchmen are likely to make a good fight of it.

William   How very tiresome of them. (*Coughs.*) So . . . we had better make sure these Northern savages do not prosper. A Scottish trading empire in the Americas, it does not bear thinking about.

Joost (*revealing a scroll*)   I have had a proclamation prepared, Sire.

William   Ah, you are useful. Read it out, then, read it out.

Joost   His Majesty's subjects are hereby commanded not to enter into any correspondence with the Scots Colony in Darien . . .

William   Good, good.

Joost   Nor to trade with them, nor to give them any assistance of any kind, whether of arms, or ammunition, or provisions or any other necessaries whatsoever.

William   Very good.

Joost   Any vessel of the English nation entering a port belonging to the Scots colonists will be in contempt of His Majesty's command, and the perpetrators will at their utmost peril be made to answer for it.

William   Hm. Yes. That will do it, I think. (*Signs it.*)

Scene Seven – Darien

A **Boy** *is alone on the beach. Maybe another* **Colonist** *performs a simple dance during it.*

Song No. 18   The Lonesome Sea

Sailor Boy   *There was a Scottish ship*
And she sailed in the morn
And the name of that ship
Was the mighty Unicorn
Oh, she sailed upon

That lonely, lonesome water
Oh, she sailed upon that lonely sea.

Up stepped a cabin boy
Saying what'll you give to me
If I climb to the topsail
In a show of bravery?
If I climb above
That lonely, lonesome water
If I climb above that lonely sea.

The captain said to him
Oh, I have some gold
And I will give a sovereign
To a lad that's truly bold
And who'll climb above
That lonely, lonesome water
Who will climb above that lonely sea.

Instrumental break.

So the cabin boy climbed up
And he overcame his fear
And when he reached the top sail
All the crew began to cheer
As they sailed upon
That lonely, lonesome water
As they sailed upon that lonely sea.

And they wondered if he'd fall
From the rigging to the deck
For they knew that if he did
He would surely break his neck
As they sailed upon
That lonely, lonesome water
As they sailed upon that lonely sea.

But the boy came safely down
And the captain kept his word
And the cabin boy was cheered
By everyone on board

As they sailed upon
That lonely, lonesome water
As they sailed upon that lonely sea.

Instrumental break

And that night the cabin boy
To his shipmates softly said
Oh I fear I have the fever
By the morning he was dead
And they dropped him in
That lonely, lonesome water
They dropped him in that lonely sea.
He was buried in
That lonely lonesome water
He was buried in the lonely sea.

The **Boy** *leaves.* **Paterson** *emerges from one of the huts, followed by* **Mrs Paterson**.

Paterson   This is foolishness. You are not well. There is no need for you to sleep in these huts when you can be in the ship's cabin. It is healthier there.

Mrs Paterson   You sleep in the cabin, I will also sleep in the cabin.

Paterson   I cannot do that.

Mrs Paterson   Then nor can I.

Paterson (*enraged*)   This is an order, woman!

Mrs Paterson   Will. You know that never works with me. (*Walks away.*)

Mackenzie *enters, followed by a French sea captain,* **Aguillon**. **Paterson** *looks up.*

Mackenzie   Mr Paterson. This is Captain Aggy-on

Aguillon (*corrects pronounciation*)   Aguillon.

Mackenzie   Aggy-on.

Aguillon   Alexandre Aguillon. Master of the Saint Philippe.

Erskine *arrives, listens.*

Mackenzie   Just dropped anchor in the bay.

Paterson   William Paterson. Councillor of the Scottish Colony of Caledonia.

Aguillon (*mocking*)   Caledonia, eh? Is that what you call it?

Erskine   You are trading on this coast?

Aguillon   Yes. But not with you.

Paterson   Why not? We have need of many items. Victuals above all.

Aguillon   Your King has issued a proclamation forbidding any man to trade with your Colony. He is not a man who easily forgives those who ignore his wishes.

Mackenzie   This cannot be true. Can this be true? Mr Paterson?

Paterson *is stunned.*

Aguillon   Why would I lie about this?

Paterson   It is what I feared. I feared it.

Aguillon   What you should fear more is the Spaniard. They know about your settlement here.

Mackenzie   But they lack the strength to attack us.

Aguillon   You are not aware they have three ships of fifty guns each newly come from Spain.

Paterson   You have seen these?

Aguillon   I have. And there is a second Spanish fleet at Carthagena, consisting of three sail: one of fifty guns, one of thirty guns and one of twenty-four guns. You should be prepared for an attack.

Paterson   I am grateful. Thank you, Captain.

Mackenzie   There is more.

Aguillon   The Indians say the Spaniards are marching
from Panama towards Darien. With a great number of men.
Their advance party has already reached Toubacanti. That
is only a day's march away.

Erskine   The Indians. They lie all the time. They change
sides all the time. They are not to be relied upon.

Aguillon   This is not my experience. That is all I have to
tell you.

Mackenzie   You will stay? Eat and drink with us?

Aguillon   No, I will weigh anchor while the wind is still fair.
It's an interesting bay you have chosen for your harbour.
Easy to sail into but given the prevailing winds on this coast,
not easy to sail out of I would think. I have heard the
Spanish tried occupying this place some two hundred years
ago. I wonder why they decided to leave? (*Makes to leave.*)

Paterson   Wait. You're a man who's taken risks in his life.
Nobody need know that you have traded with us. You have
victuals on board?

Aguillon   Yes. But you have nothing of value to offer me in
return.

Paterson   Yes, we do. Of course we do. Mackenzie?

Mackenzie   I'm sure we can offer items that –

Paterson   There is certainly trade to be done between us.

Aguillon   Mr Paterson. I have seen what you have to offer.
And I must tell you I have no interest in acquiring three
hundred wigs. Nor five hundred pairs of knitted hosiery.
Nor even two thousand slightly mildewed Scottish
catechisms. It may surprise you to know that in Catholic
France there is no great demand for Protestant prayer
books. Good day, gentlemen. (*Makes to go.*)

Paterson   One moment. You came ashore merely to provide us with information? From the goodness of your heart?

Aguillon   In a way. You see, my grandfather came from Scotland – but wisely chose to live in France. Your colony is a ridiculous venture, but I have no desire to see you wiped out. I fear I am a foolish and sentimental man. Though being only one quarter Scottish, not as foolish and sentimental as yourselves. Good day to you. (*Leaves.*)

The three men absorb the information in silence.

Paterson   We could be attacked at any time. And the fort is still not built, Mr Erskine.

Erskine   If we get the twelve-pounders mounted on the escarpment, and complete the defences to the landward, then –

Paterson   We should certainly do that. And with all haste. But I have another suggestion. You may find it too bold.

Erskine   I may not.

Mackenzie   What is it?

Paterson   The Spanish will have spies along the coast. They will know that we are fortifying the town. So what will they least expect?

Erskine   What?

Paterson   They will least expect *us* to attack *them* . . . If we fall upon their vanguard at Toubacanti we can defeat them by force of numbers alone. When King William hears that we can defeat the Spaniard in battle he will soon realise that we are now a trading nation alongside England, a trading nation and a military power, and no royal proclamation is going to put an end to us. Mr Mackenzie. Make an announcement. Let the entire colony know that Caledonia stands ready to fight! Let the *world* know that Caledonia stands ready to fight!

Scene Eight – a living room in Edinburgh

Early morning in a darkened room.

Blackwood *and* **Balfour** *are found slumped over a table, amidst empty bottles and glasses and remains of food. A* **Servant** *enters, open the shutters, clears up a bit. Light floods in.* **Balfour** *and* **Blackwood** *groan and stir.*

Servant (*to audience*)   Ladies and gentlemen. There now follows a bit of a cliché: two Scotsmen with a hangover. This is to illustrate the even-handedness of the play. Having unfairly portrayed the English, the French, the Dutch, the Germans and the Danes, it seems only right and proper to do the same for the Scots. Thank you.

Blackwood   What hour is it?

Servant   Ten.

Blackwood   Bring us coffee.

Balfour   Chocolate. Cups of chocolate.

Blackwood   Coffee.

Balfour   Chocolate.

Blackwood   Coffee.

Servant   I'll bring both, eh?

Balfour   Ten o'clock . . . We'll be late for the Company meeting.

Servant   Few are stirring in the town, sir. Last night all of Edinburgh was celebrating. We saw off the Spaniard, sir, did we not? I hear they are striking special silver plate to mark the Scottish victory at the Battle of Toubacanti.

Blackwood   Aye, aye, a great victory. Coffee.

Balfour   And chocolate.

Servant   Yes, sir. (*Leaves.*)

Blackwood (*derisively*)   Great victory. The Battle of Toubacanti. It was a but a skirmish. Three Spanish dead and two Scots.

Balfour   That is a victory.

Blackwood   Aye, maybe, but it scarcely merits a night of revelry and rioting. And it was all but four months ago. Who knows what may have happend since? The Spaniard may be more powerful than we thought.

Balfour   It was we who declared it a victory.

Blackwood   People were in need of good news.

Balfour   Yes. (*Looks at bottles.*) How many bottles of claret did we drink last night?

Blackwood   Well, I had two and . . . and you must have had three. (*Counts the empty bottles.*)

Balfour   Mr Blackwood, that makes five.

Blackwood   Yes.

Balfour   How many empty bottles are there?

Blackwood   Six. Oh. I see what you mean. You must have drunk four. Where's my coffee?

Balfour   I do not comprehend how you can swallow yon abominable heathenish liquid.

Blackwood   Coffee fuels the intellectual discourse of our nation, Mr Balfour.

Balfour   Intellectual discourse? When did you last take part in intellectual discourse, Mr Blackwood?

Blackwood   Um, let me see . . .

The **Servant** *enters with a cup of coffee and a cup of hot chocolate and places them on the table.*

Balfour   Hmmm. Now listen. We know Toubacanti was not the great victory that the rabble believe it to be. But it will enable us to make another call for funds.

Blackwood   Aye, that's true. There'll be no shortage of investment now.

Servant *withdraws.*

Balfour   We'll not let the English strangle our colony with their embargo. We'll equip and provision a second fleet. A fleet even mightier than the first. And if it sails from the Clyde instead of from Leith the voyage will be shortened by three weeks, maybe four.

Blackwood   It can reach Darien in . . . in . . . a little over two months.

Balfour   Very good, Mr Blackwood, very good. In no time at all you'll be able to count up to six.

Blackwood   We will make the nation proud of our heroic lads fighting overseas.

Balfour   Aye, soon enough the people will have more good news than they know what to do with.

They simultaneously reach for their coffee and their chocolate and sip.

Balfour & Blackwood   Ahhhhh.

Scene Nine – a hut in Darien

Paterson *is talking to the* **Colonists**, *several of whom are writing down what he says.*

Paterson (*dictating*)   One of . . . the . . . most fruitfullest . . . . spots of ground . . . on . . . the face . . . of the earth.

First Colonist   Are we obliged to write this exactly as you say it, Mr Paterson?

Paterson   No. If instead you wish to tell them about the swamps, and the fevers, and the depredations, and the hunger, then by all means, tell them. Tell them that we bury a dozen men a day. Tell them that New Edinburgh is but a row of straw huts. Tell that Fort St Andrew is but a half-built palisade placed upon a stinking marsh. Let tales of death and disaster circulate in Scotland. Let them think that we are half-drowned rats not worth saving. Let all of Scotland know that the Spaniard is more powerful than we thought and may soon attack us in overwhelming numbers. And when because of your wretched accounts of our great endeavour they decide to build no more ships and our needful supplies are not sent and we succumb to hunger and despair, come to me and say you are proud of what you wrote.

First Colonist   Sir, I only wish to recount the truth of our situation.

Paterson   The truth? The truth? Damn you and your truth. Your truth won't warm your grave. Let me have the truth of your courage. The truth of your resolution. The truth of your faith in God. The truth of your faith in Caledonia.

First Colonist   Yes, sir.

Second Colonist   Sir, many of us are unlettered. If somebody could –

Paterson (*pointing at* **First Colonist**)   He'll write your letters for you. (*To* **First Colonist**.) Will you not?

First Colonist   Yes, sir.

Paterson   And you'll know what to say, will you not?

First Colonist   Yes, sir.

Paterson *walks away. They wait until he is out of earshot.*

First Colonist (*quietly*)   Tell me what you truly want to say and I will write it for you.

Second Colonist   Thank you. Say . . . write this down . . . I . . . I don't know if I will see my homeland again. We live on two pounds of flour a week. That's two pounds by the Company weighing, which means one pound only.

Unnoticed by them **Pennicuick** *approaches.*

First Colonist   Slow down, slow down.

Second Colonist   And the flour must be sifted to remove the maggots . . .

Pennicuick   What are these lies?

They try to hide the letter. **Pennicuick** *snatches it, reads it.*

Pennicuick   Lies, lies.

Second Colonist   They are not lies, captain. The flour we are given is full of maggots.

First Colonist   Aye, and sometimes there's no flour at all and we get a handful of dried peas instead and when we boil them up we have first to skim the worms off the top.

Third Colonist *comes over and joins them.*

Second Colonist   And for all this short allowance we are every man daily turned out to work with hatchet, or pick-axe, or shovel, and continue until night. Sometimes we work all day up to the top of our breeches in water.

Pennicuick   You are grown soft.

Third Colonist (*pulling shirt off shoulder*)   Look, just take a look at that, Captain . . . My shoulder is so wore with carrying burdens that the skin has come off it and grown full of boils.

Pennicuick (*turns away in disgust*)   I do not wish to know about your boils, sir. They stink. I suggest you all get back to work.

Third Colonist   What do you know of work, Captain? You who lie at ease in the cabins of your ships. You and the other Councillors.

Second Colonist   Not Mr Paterson.

Third Colonist   Not Mr Paterson, no. But all the rest of you. Keeping the best food and drink for yourselves.

First Colonist   Why is a man who is sick and obliged to stay within the huts given no food?

Second Colonist   The governance of this colony has been compassed about with lies.

Third Colonist   We should not have come here. It is not probable that one Scotsman in twenty could live here, the place is unwholesome.

Second Colonist   Three hundred graves, Captain Pennicuick. Three hundred graves. And every day a dozen more.

They begin to gather round him, threateningly.

First Colonist   Three hundred graves.

Third Colonist   Three hundred graves.

It becomes a sort of chant perhaps reinforced with pre-recorded voices. **Paterson** *has appeared at one side. He watches and listens.*

Colonists   Three hundred graves. Three hundred graves. Three hundred graves. Three hundred graves. Three hundred graves . . .

Triumphal music from the next scene creeps in.

Scene Ten – a hill overlooking the Clyde estuary

Triumphal music.
Balfour *and* **Blackwood** *watch the second fleet depart.*
Off: cheering.
Blackwood *points and checks off the ships in a ledger as each one is sighted.*

Blackwood   The Rising Sun.

Balfour   She's a beauty.

Blackwood   She is that.

Balfour   She cost us a pretty penny of course. More than the rest of the fleet put together. We can be proud,

Mr Blackwood, we can be proud. A second great fleet
to join the first. Does it not make your heart beat a little
faster?

Blackwood   Aye, it does. Look. The Hamilton. She's a
beauty too.

Balfour   A fine sight, a fine sight. All in all a glorious sight.
Enough to stir the heart of the sourest Scot, and God knows
there are plenty of them about. I never knew the Clyde
could look so bonny. Almost as bonny as the Forth. Who'd
have thought it, eh?

Blackwood (*points*)   And there comes the Bo'ness.

Balfour   Aye, look at yon ships. Bearing one thousand
three hundred men, women and children on their way to a
new and better life.

Blackwood   And look, over there, the Hope.

Balfour   Four mighty ships, Mr Blackwood, four mighty
ships. Carrying the spirit of Scotland. When they reach
Darien and join up with the first expedition we will be as
powerful a presence in the Americas as any nation on the
face of the earth. Darien will bring wealth, and power and
glory to Scotland. Never again will we have to bend our
knee to the English. The Lord God has smiled upon this
little nation of ours, and made us great.

Blackwood   We are blessed, Mr Balfour, we are blessed.

They leave.

Scene Eleven – Darien

On Darien **Erskine**, **Pennicuik** *and* **Paterson** *are locked in grim
conflict.* **Paterson** *is ill.*

Paterson   You are giving up! You are all giving up on me.
You are like mice. Did you think our great endeavour would

be easy? Did you? Where's the fight in you? What are you made of? Milk and curds? Dear God, why am I surrounded by poor weak feeble creatures such as you?!

Erskine   How can we build a trading colony if nobody will trade with us?

Pennicuik (*drinking*)   Erskine's right. The King's proclamation has finished us. But it allows us to abandon the Colony with our honour intact.

Paterson   You cannot have intact what you never had to start with.

Pennicuik   By God, Paterson, you're a rude bugger. (*Holding up an empty glass.*) Boy! More wine! Where is that boy?

Paterson   He is dead.

Pennicuik   Oh.

Erskine   We'll receive no more provisions from home. No more ships. No more help. They're afraid of the King. Scotland has given up on us.

Paterson   We don't know that. Ships may be on their way.

Erskine   I'll tell you what ships are on their way. Spanish ships. Seven of them, standing off the coast. And a Spanish army approaching by land.

Pennicuick   If we surrender now, we may still escape with our lives. What we cannot do is just sit here waiting and hoping. With so many men dead. So many ill. So many suffering.

Paterson   Since when did you care about the men?

Penniciuk   You're not looking so well yourself, Paterson.

Erskine   We have to leave.

Pennicucik   Aye, if the Spanish press home and attack we're all dead. Let us capitulate with honour. (*Empties his bottle.*)

Erskine, **Pennicuick** *and the other* **Colonists** *leave.* **Paterson** *is shaking and sweating. He falls to his knees.* **Mrs Paterson** *enters, kneels down beside him.*

Paterson   It can't be done. It can't be done. It can't be done.

Mrs Paterson   Will . . . it is all right. We will go home.

Paterson   Where I shall face shame and dishonour.

Mrs Paterson   All you have done, you've done with honour. There is no shame.

Paterson   It can't be done.

Mackenzie *appears. He waits, watches.*

Mackenzie (*gently*)   Mr Paterson . . . Mrs Paterson . . . I am sorry . . . The Spanish have landed. Their commander will grant us safe passage. But we must leave now.

Slowly **Paterson** *and* **Mrs Paterson** *get up and leave. As* **Mackenzie** *leaves, upstage of him a huge graveyard of crude wooden crosses is revealed.*

In a ghostly faint form we hear singing off.

Song No. 19   Time To Be Bold (Reprise)

Sailors   *Time to be bold, me lads,*
                            Time to be bold,
                            Time to think of better times to come.
                            Think about the gold, me lads,
                            Think about the gold . . .

Scene Twelve – the Port of Leith/Edinburgh

Nine of the **Nameless** *enter, half-singing, half-whispering. Each is carrying a wreath.*

Song No. 20   Trade Begets Trade (Reprise)

The Nameless   *Trade begets trade*
                    Money makes money

> *Wealth creates wealth*
> *Riches from riches*
> *Piled upon riches*
> *Unto the end of the world.*

Paterson *enters, head bowed.*

The **Nameless** *each declare the name of the ship, as a wreath is thrown into the sea for each ship.*

First Nameless   The Unicorn. Abandoned in New England.

Second Nameless   The St Andrew. Abandoned in Jamaica.

Third Nameless   The Dolphin. Lost to the Spanish.

First Nameless   The Endeavour. Sunk in the Caribbean.

Second Nameless   The Hope. Wrecked off Cuba.

Third Nameless   The Bo'ness. Surrendered to the Spanish.

First Nameless   The Duke of Hamilton. Sunk in Charleston Harbour.

Second Nameless   The Rising Sun. Sunk in a hurricane with the loss of all hands.

First Nameless   The Caledonia. The only ship to return to Scotland.

Blackwood (*entering*)   The climate was to blame.

Balfour (*entering*)   The English were to blame.

Mackenzie (*entering*)   The Spaniard was to blame.

Erskine (*entering*)   William Paterson was to blame.

Paterson   I know. I know.

Their gaze follows him as he leaves.

Scene Thirteen – St Giles Cathedral, Edinburgh

Borland *appears in the pulpit. His voice echoes round the cold stone walls.*

Borland   The General Assembly of Church of Scotland has taken to heart the many tokens of God's displeasure that are gone forth against this land. We see with sadness the blasting of the undertakings of this nation in the colony of Caledonia, together with the loss of two thousand of our countrymen . . . and a great part of the nation's treasure. We have cause to infer that our sins must be great and heinous in the sight of God. And great has been God's punishment. I saw the suffering. As our ships fled Darien I went below decks among the sick to visit them in their sad and dying condition, their noisome stench choking and suffocating. Malignant fevers and the flux swept away great numbers. I saw with my own eyes and heard with my own ears the last tormented moments of wretched sinners as they prepared to enter through the gates of hell. Too late for regrets. Too late for repentance. Each man paying for his mortal mistakes, as Scotland must now pay for hers. Surely it is a sign of God's wrath that a second great fleet should have been sent to Darien when the colony had already been abandoned and that it too should have been destroyed upon the high seas. It is obvious to every discerning eye that this land is filled with wickedness and abominations among persons of all ranks and degrees. And instead of repenting of our sins and renewing our engagements unto God, the most part of our people have given themselves over unto jollity and wantonness. Upon all these considerations this Assembly has thought fit to declare for the nation a day of solemn fasting and humiliation and the exercise of sincere and unfeigned repentance for the sins that abound in our land.

Scene Fourteen – the offices of the Company of Scotland

In a ritualised sequence, the **Directors** *of the Company round on* **Paterson**.

Balfour   I want my money back, Mr Paterson.

Erskine   I want my money back, Mr Paterson.

Blackwood   I want my money back, Mr Paterson.

Borland   I want my money back, Mr Paterson.

Mackenzie   Mr Paterson, I have not been paid.

Balfour   My business is destroyed, Mr Paterson.

Erskine   Your reputation is destroyed, Mr Paterson.

Blackwood   Our future is destroyed, Mr Paterson.

Borland   Scotland is destroyed, Mr Paterson.

Mackenzie   And I have not been paid.

Balfour   I want my money back, Mr Paterson.

Erskine   I want my money back, Mr Paterson.

Blackwood   I want my money back, Mr Paterson.

Borland   I want my money back, Mr Paterson.

Mackenzie   And I have not been paid.

Paterson, *defeated, walks off as they stare after him.*

Scene Fifteen – The Court of King Willam

The **King** *is having tea. He is clearly unwell.*

Joost   Mr William Paterson!

Paterson (*bows*)   Your Majesty.

William   You never really go away, do you Paterson? How long now since you set forth on your foolish adventure in Panama?

Paterson   Nigh on four years, Sire.

William   And here you are. A failure. A wretched man who brought disaster upon his wretched land. I assume you live here in London now?

Paterson   No, Sire. In Scotland.

William   How very brave of you. Do the common people not wish to do terrible things to you?

Paterson   The common people do not present a problem, Sire. The shareholders of the Company of Scotland present a problem.

William   Ah.

Paterson   They are a barrier to the union of our two nations.

William   Why?

Paterson   Many of them sit in Parliament. If they feel cheated, they will vote against any treaty of union.

William   But they were not cheated by me, Mr Paterson, they were cheated by you. Thanks to you they lost every penny. Scotland is finished as an independent nation. Don't they know that?

Paterson   I know it, Sire. I know Scotland cannot prosper as an independent nation. We need the financial power of England. That is the lesson of Darien.

William   Oh, I thought the lesson of Darien was don't give your money to bankers.

Paterson   Sire. The treaty that is being envisaged requires Scotland to take on a part of England's national debt. It is a vast sum. It is an unbearable sum to impose upon Scotland.

It means union with England will never be accepted. They will not swallow it, Sire.

William   They must. I may not live to see it, but I already know that union is inevitable.

Paterson   It is not, I assure you, Sire. There may still be years of negotiation ahead before union comes about. During that time, Scottish resentment against England can only increase. His Majesty's embargo on trade with our colony dealt us a fatal blow.

William   Oh come, come. Darien was simply the worng place to go. You are looking for an excuse. How easy it is for you Scots always to blame the English.

Paterson   Your Majesty must understand that others may tell him what he wishes to hear. From me he will hear only the truth.

William   I cannot allow Scotland to escape its share of the national debt. The English Parliament would not countenance it.

Paterson   There may be another way to solve it, Sire.

William   How?

Paterson (*tentatively*)   Well . . . if England were to offer a cash sum . . . A sum that is equivalent to Scotland's share of the national debt . . . That could be . . . helpful.

William   Why should England do that? It makes no sense. We are meant to take from Scotland with one hand and give it back with the other?

Paterson   You would not be giving it back to Scotland, Sire. Not exactly.

William   So to whom would we be giving this . . . 'cash sum'?

Paterson   To the directors and shareholders of the Company of Scotland. To compensate those who lost their money in the Darien venture.

William   Why?

Paterson   Many of them wield great influence. Indeed, many sit in the Scottish Parliament. If they are compensated, they will be inclined to favour a treaty of union. And vote for it.

William   You are proposing a bribe.

Paterson   I am proposing compensation.

William   I am to compensate them for every penny of their losses, is that what you propose?

Paterson   Yes. Plus interest.

William   Plus interest?

Paterson   Yes. Everything they lost. Plus fifty per cent. Sire.

William   You are very bold, Paterson. Are you not?

Paterson   Your Majesty wishes to see England and Scotland united as one nation. Does he not?

William (*thinks*)   The Company of Scotland . . . I am told you have plans for new colonies?

Paterson   I have.

William   If the English Parliament agrees to your proposition . . .

Paterson   Your Majesty will put it to them?

William   I may. But following union, we cannot allow the Company of Scotland to continue. Any treaty would have to ensure the Company of Scotland is dissolved.

Paterson   I would find that most regrettable.

William   I suspect you will get over it. You will always devise some new scheme to make money, Paterson, I know the sort of man you are. With every passing day I encounter more and more men such as you.

Paterson   I beg your Majesty not to dissolve the Company of Scotland.

William   It is decided.

Paterson   But –

William   Do not argue with me, sir. Your shareholders will be compensated, they will help to bring about union, and your wretched trading company will be closed down. Not another word from you, sir, not another word! Joost. Hunting. I fear I am too ill.

Paterson *bows as* **William** *and* **Joost** *leave. He straightens up with a smile of triumph on his face.*

Scene Sixteen – a street in Edinburgh

A cart laden with banknotes, gold and silver coin is pulled onto the stage, protected by English Dragoons. Coins and notes spill out on to the ground.

Song No. 21   They Sent It Up From London

The Nameless   *They sent it up from London*
With soldiers either side
The money
The money
The money
The money always follows the money
And poverty has no place left to hide.

The directors all make money
The investors all make money
Oh and we almost forgot to mention
William Paterson
Pleads poverty
And gets a pension.
How nice to have a pension.

A few years later
The money that's left over
Is handed to a brand new institution . . . .

*A **Banker** from the early eighteen century comes on, makes a little formal speech.*

Banker   And so in conclusion, to our investors I would say this: to no establishment could our money and trust be with more propriety confided than to our eminent offspring . . . the Royal Bank of Scotland.

The Nameless   *They brought it through the high street*
One sunny day in June
The money
The money
The money always follows the money
And he who pays the piper calls the tune.

*A **Piper** enters and plays a lament as the gold is shovelled and the banknotes unloaded.*

The Nameless   Thomas Dalrymple, planter. Dead of the fever.

Charles Hamilton, midshipman. Dead of the flux.

Jacob Yorkland, volunteer. Dead of the flux.

James Davidson, planter. Dead of the fever.

Henry Charters, volunteer. Dead of the flux.

Adam Hill, planter. Dead of the flux.

Walter Eliot, midshipman. Dead of the fever.

David Henderson, sailor. Dead of the flux.

Andrew Brown, cabin boy. Drowned.

Lieutenant Hugh Hay.

Robert Gaudie, planter.

James Montgomerie, sailor.

John Malbon, merchant,

Margaret Paterson, wife of William Paterson.

The music dies.

The **Piper** *withdraws.* **Paterson** *crosses the stage, head bowed, carrying a single wooden cross. The* **Nameless** *whisper/chant the next song.*

Song No. 22   Make A List (Reprise)

The Nameless   *When there's nothing must be missed*
Make a list
Make a list
Get the world around you under your control.
To make sure that you exist
Make a list
Make a list
Make a list . . . .

George Menzies, planter.

Walter Johnson, surgeon's mate.

John Aird, planter.

Henry Grapes, trumpeter.

Peter Telfer, planter.

John Burrell, sailor.

Daniel Martin, sailor.

Lieutenant James Inglis.

William McClellan, boy.

Song No. 23   Trade Begets Trade (Reprise)

Paterson   *Trade begets trade*

All   *Trade begets trade*

Paterson   *Money makes money*

All   *Money makes money*

Paterson   *Wealth creates wealth*

All   *Wealth creates wealth*
                        Riches from riches
                        Piled upon riches
                        To the end of the world.

*Banknotes descend upon the heads of the audience. On each
banknote is written the name of a colonist who died.*

Curtain.

Printed in the USA
CPSIA information can be obtained
at www.ICGtesting.com
LVHW020845171024
794056LV00002B/403